BE
STRONG
— AND —
TAKE HEART

BE STRONG
AND — TAKE HEART

40 DAYS TO A
HOPE-FILLED LIFE

ZONDERVAN

Be Strong and Take Heart
Copyright © 2019 by Zondervan

Requests for information should be addressed to:
Zondervan, *3900 Sparks Dr. SE, Grand Rapids, Michigan 49546*

Print ISBN 978-0-310-76739-8

Ebook ISBN 978-0-310-76764-0

Scripture quotations are taken from the Holy Bible, New International Version®, NIV®. Copyright © 1973, 1978, 1984, 2011 by Biblica, Inc.® Used by permission of Zondervan. All rights reserved worldwide. www.Zondervan.com. The "NIV" and "New International Version" are trademarks registered in the United States Patent and Trademark Office by Biblica, Inc.®

Any internet addresses (websites, blogs, etc.) and telephone numbers in this book are offered as a resource. They are not intended in any way to be or imply an endorsement by Zondervan, nor does Zondervan vouch for the content of these sites and numbers for the life of this book.

Published in association with the Books & Such Literary Management, 52 Mission Circle, Suite 122, PMB 170, Santa Rosa, California 95409-5370. www.booksandsuch.com.

Contributor: Ashley N. Mays
Interior design: Denise Froehlich

Printed in China

19 20 21 22 23 / DSC / 10 9 8 7 6 5 4 3 2 1

PART ONE

My Heart

What Is My Heart? Why Does It Matter?

Jesus replied: "'Love the Lord your God with all your heart and with all your soul and with all your mind.' This is the first and greatest commandment. And the second is like it: 'Love your neighbor as yourself.'"

MATTHEW 22:37–39

Your heart beats around 100,000 times a day. In that same twenty-four-hour period, it pumps nearly 2,000 gallons of blood throughout your body to keep you alive. This fantastic muscle relies on tiny electrical impulses to help it stay in rhythm. When those impulses don't quite line up, it beats too quickly or too slowly. That's a problem.

When a problem with our heart exists, we have to pay attention because our very lives depend on its well-being.

Our spiritual heart—the heart that gets a workout when we love and when we grieve, when we serve and when we sin—is gloriously intricate and every bit as purposeful as our literal heart.

Your spiritual heart is a unique piece of your identity, built into you from the very beginning to help you know and love God, others, and yourself better.

Have you ever felt such passion for a cause that it couldn't be ignored? Or have you ever cried with a friend over a fresh loss? Maybe you've sat in silent prayer, only to have a vivid sense of God's love wash over you. These, and so many other experiences, result from the life-giving rhythms of our spiritual hearts.

When the Pharisees, the law-lovers of ancient times, asked Jesus what the most important law was, he answered them by saying, "Love the Lord your God with all your heart, with all your soul, and with all your mind. And love your neighbor as yourself."

Jesus didn't say these things because he thought they sounded right or because they would look nice painted on the side of the temple wall. He said them because it was a well-known part of the Torah, scriptures the Pharisees would have been able to recite as teachers of the law.

Even though the Pharisees were teachers, even though they already knew the words and seemed to know it all, and even though they were often considered the ones to go to with questions about spiritual things, Jesus knew they needed the reminder as much as anyone else.

Just because we study the Bible a lot and we've learned the words, that doesn't mean we live those words well. To live them well, we have to be willing to live with a little bit of a mess.

When a surgeon does open-heart surgery, she doesn't expect to stay clean. She wears surgical scrubs and a cap, multiple pairs of gloves, and protective eyewear. If she waltzed into the operating room in an evening gown and a sleek pair of Louboutins, and then got upset when a drop of blood spilled on her dress, we'd have a lot of questions, like: Why was she wearing an evening gown to operate? If she didn't want to get messy, why did she study and train to be a heart surgeon? Didn't she realize the mess wasn't something to fight against, but something to expect and prepare for?

Sadly, these Pharisees weren't the kind of people who were well prepared for spiritual heart surgery. Instead, they were the ones who got offended when the heart work got a little messy.

So offended, in fact, that they ended up crucifying Jesus because of it.

Letting Jesus take over our hearts gets messy sometimes. We'll have questions even as we try to trust God. Living as a Christ follower in a world full of scary situations and hurting people is hard. If our hearts aren't anchored—tied down—to the truth of God's love, faithfulness, and care for us, it can be easy to become offended, angry, and closed off.

The good news is, Jesus already did the hard work of becoming a sacrifice to pay for our sins, work that was impossible for us to do. Now we must do the hard work of pursuing God and training our hearts to turn to him during times of joy and times of crisis. And when we feel ourselves veering off course, we can lean into God's heart. We can lean into serving others. And we can lean into the uniqueness of our own hearts.

We'll have to muddle through messes at times, of course. But the journey toward a heart that's fully alive will also be infused with hope, trust, light, and joy. The gifts God gives us when we pursue him with our whole hearts are worth uncertainty right now, because we can be confident in his love.

Remember: God is the one who makes beauty from messes. He can take your heart and bring you into the fullness and beauty of all he intended you to be.

Live

What are you carrying around in your heart today? There are probably some good things and some hard things. Write down the first five things that come to mind. There aren't any right or wrong answers when it comes to your heart—after God, you're the one who knows it best! And no judgment if you're carrying more heavy than happy things around right now. Sometimes that's how life is. But make a commitment not to let the mess of doing heart work scare you off. God isn't afraid of the mess, so you don't have to be either!

Pray

Jesus, I'm afraid of learning what it looks like to love you, the people I see every day, and myself with my whole heart. It's a lot easier to stay where I am. Give me the courage to leave behind what feels okay for what you've promised is great. Teach me how to exchange an unhealthy heart for a strong one. I ask you to do the work that my heart needs so I can become the woman you intended me to be, a woman who knows your heart and represents you so well that others are drawn to you.

Think

My heart doesn't need to fight against the messy process of growing; instead, it can stay steadfast through the journey and look forward to the end result.

The Care and Keeping of My Heart

You will seek me and find me when you seek me with all your heart.

JEREMIAH 29:13

If you wanted to start a thriving garden in your yard, what would be the best way to begin? Would you go to a greenhouse or a hardware store to pick out flowers? Or would you begin even earlier in the process by purchasing seed packets?

Those are several necessary steps to take when planting a garden, for sure. The result would probably be a decent garden by the end of the growing season. The flowers would still look beautiful. There would be a few tomatoes on the vine or blueberries on the bush.

But if, before the planting even started, you began saving your banana peels, your coffee grounds, and your egg shells to put in the compost bin, a few months later you'd have a nutrient-dense compost supply ready to go. When the compost was ready, you'd spread it around in the soil. After the soil had been well prepared, then you'd choose your plants and continue gardening, using compost wherever the plants would need to take root.

There wouldn't be a noticeable difference between the plants in pre-prepared, compost-rich soil and the plants that were simply plopped into the ground before growing season started. Once springtime arrived, though, the plants that had been put in the nourished environment would have brighter, fuller leaves.

Any flowers would have more blooms, and they'd be stronger and healthier. The produce would yield a greater, tastier harvest.

Our spiritual hearts have a lot in common with gardens. If we want to experience God more fully, we have to tend our hearts more intentionally. Without any prep, we can still see him. He'll continue to be present in our lives, and we can still have a relationship with him. But we might not get to experience the full extent of the gifts he gives us because we aren't paying close attention.

"Fertilizing" the soil of our spiritual hearts happens when we choose to be intentional. We take action to get to know God better, and that action helps us to grow closer to his heart. Here's what that looks like when we live it out:

We spend time reading the Bible. This is especially important, even if we go to church or a Christian school and hear about God from others. God's Word is one of the ways he directly speaks to each one of us. If we don't make time to personally read the Bible, we lose out on hearing what he has to say.

We memorize verses that stand out to us, so we can reflect on what they mean throughout the day. We can't always carry our Bibles around with us, and even if we *do* have a copy nearby, there are times where we can't simply look up a verse, like if we're working, or taking a test, or doing something that requires us to be fully present. If we've memorized Scripture, God will bring those words to mind when we need to remember his nearness or his faithfulness in the middle of a difficult moment. Memorizing Bible verses is one way we can write his love and faithfulness on our hearts so it will come back to us when we need it.

We pray, taking time to voice our questions, concerns, and thankfulness. We also listen. Prayer is a conversation with the almighty Creator of all things. How awesome is it that we have the freedom to talk to him whenever we want? There's nobody else in the entire universe we have that privilege to do that with except God.

Also, not only do we get to talk to God, he listens to what we have to say and then *he answers.* Sometimes God chooses to answer our prayers by taking care of the stuff going on, and sometimes he chooses to nudge our hearts in a different direction. But if we aren't taking the time to pray and listen, we might miss out on those nudges or we might not realize when an answer to prayer is unfolding right in front of our eyes.

We confess the gross stuff we're holding on to. Nothing will blot out our ability to see God's goodness like having a death grip on sin. And it's just that—a death grip, locking our fingers around something that will lead to death. God already knows about the thing we're gripping, and he doesn't bludgeon us with guilt to get us to clear the air. Instead, he holds his arms wide open and waits for us to remember the freedom he's already provided.

We enjoy the uniqueness of our personhood. God made us who we are for a reason. If we enjoy being outside in nature, we can connect with God there. If our passions include art and creativity, God can meet us there too. Whatever they are, the things that bring tears of joy to our eyes are gifts to enjoy. Why wouldn't God hang out with us in those moments too?

We stick it out in the hard times, and ask tough questions instead of giving up. Terribly difficult things happen in the world, and they even happen to people who love and follow Jesus. It is an unfortunate reality of living in a fallen world, and sometimes it's overwhelming.

God isn't afraid of our hard situations or our hurting hearts. Even when we feel lonely, angry, or terrified, he doesn't move farther away. Sometimes he even chooses to bless us in super special ways, sending us love notes that settle deeply into our hearts. We have to keep watching for those love notes, though, because if we've turned away, we might miss that extra sprinkle of grace.

We teach ourselves to remember thankfulness. When life isn't unicorns and glitter, we forget the many ways we've already been blessed. Our minds and hearts don't always have excellent long-term memory skills. Start keeping a list of all the ways you've been blessed (and not in the Instagram hashtag way). These are *real* blessings, the ways you've felt cared for, seen, and known, and all the other things that make you feel truly alive.

This isn't an exhaustive list of ways to grow closer to God, and it's certainly not a formula for hacking your faith to manipulate God into giving you everything you ask (that never works!). Faith and a relationship with God is a work in progress. We're always learning and always growing.

Truthfully, God loves you just as much even if you don't do *any* work to prepare your heart. It's just that, like leaving the compost out of the garden, if we don't do the heart work at each step of our own growing season, we miss having the full, blossoming gifts God can create, all because we haven't prepared and watched for what he's doing.

Live

Underline one or two "heart preparation" strategies you want to commit to for the next thirty-eight days. Can you think of any other ways you can prepare your heart so you're more aware of what God's doing in your life? Write those things down too.

Every time you experience God showing you an aspect of his character (his love for you, his faithfulness, his nearness, etc.), make note of it. When you get to the end of this devotional, look back at all the times you recognized God showing up in your life in just the last few weeks alone.

Pray

God, I want to be more aware of the ways you're already actively working in my life. Sometimes I get so distracted by all the other stuff going on that it's hard to see what you're doing. Would you show me in all sorts of ways how you're here with me, ways that are special to you and me alone? I want to experience life with you. Open my eyes so I'll recognize you and what you're doing, no matter the situation.

Think

My heart better recognizes the ways God is at work in my life when I am intentional about growing and enjoying my relationship with him.

What Does It Mean to Guard My Heart?

Do not let [my words] out of your sight, keep them within your heart; for they are life to those who find them and health to one's whole body. Above all else, guard your heart, for everything you do flows from it.

PROVERBS 4:21–23

*D*riving by a well-maintained horse farm is a beautiful experience. The lush, rolling hills, green grass, sleek horses grazing side by side, and tiny foals playing at their mothers' sides invoke a sense of peace, rest, and safety. But, of course, the peace, rest, and safety on farms like these wouldn't exist if it weren't for the miles and miles of fence around them.

Horse owners know that in order to protect the animals they love and have invested in, they need to maintain good boundaries. If the fence breaks or is damaged, they move their horses to another paddock quickly and fix the damage as soon as possible. The fences aren't there to keep the horses from enjoying their lives or to keep them from being horses; the fences are there to give the horses as much freedom as possible while protecting them from outside threats at the same time.

As one of the most valuable pieces of our God-given identities, our hearts need similar protection. Take a look at the end of Proverbs 4:23. It says *everything* we do flows from our hearts. In other words, our hearts guide how we see the world and decide to act based on that view—almost like an internal compass. If our hearts aren't tuned toward the things God wants us to follow and do, we head in the wrong directions and lose connection with the woman God created us to be. A woman without a strong, spiritually centered heart is a woman who ceases to live in the way she was intended.

But sometimes we focus on the "guard your heart" part of the verse, and we set up elaborate, high fences, rows and rows of them, in order to protect us from everything that could be harmful. *Maybe,* we think, *if I make this fence a really high wall to guard my heart, I'll never get hurt or tempted, and God will be more pleased with me.* Some of us have deep pain from family and friend drama or from failed relationships, so our walls are topped with razor wire, surrounded by a moat filled with hungry, man-eating eels.

Others of us have gone the other direction, deciding the instruction to guard our hearts is an old rule that no longer applies. We incorrectly think we're supposed to let everybody and everything in to prove how loving we are, believing that if we have any boundaries at all, we're being close-minded.

Neither of these are great options. Both keep us from having healthy hearts. And both are not truly looking at what the verse means.

The goal of guarding our hearts isn't to help us avoid heartbreak. It isn't to make sure we live pain-free lives. And it isn't about following a bunch of rules to make God happier with us. Being a good gatekeeper of our hearts means we know where our responsibilities begin and end, and we choose to let the good things in and are cautious and discerning around everything else.

But how can you best discern what is good and what may be harmful? The best example to follow is Jesus—after all, he experienced everything in this world and kept his heart perfectly tuned to God's will. Jesus often stepped outside the "lines" the Jewish people had established as hard and fast rules—for example, he relied on what God told him was right instead of what his society said was acceptable, he healed people on the Sabbath, and he went into communities that were filled with "sinners" that "good" people shouldn't spend time with. Today, that might mean looking to the Bible to check it against what people tell you is correct, not following a rule for the rule's sake, and showing God's love to people outside your close circle— even people who may not believe all the same things you do. If your heart is well-tuned toward God's will, and you set your boundaries according to your heart, you don't have to worry about getting lost or being led astray.

Be a good gatekeeper who's devoted to allowing biblical love and truth to shape your heart. Know what God says about you and learn how he feels about you by spending time with him. Take what he says about you in his Word (the Bible) and fold that into your heart. Have the courage to believe it, even though we live in a world that tells us otherwise.

Live

Review the relationships in your life. Are there people you've been afraid to let in, even though their friendship might be a source of truth and goodness in your life? What about people who often push past your boundaries? Evaluate the people you're currently allowing to have a voice in your life and decide where the healthy boundaries are in each situation.

Pray

Holy Spirit, I look to you as the ultimate gatekeeper of my heart. You know better than I do what is true and what needs

to be reevaluated. Give me wisdom as I look at my relationships, my thoughts, and my feelings. Help me let go of the things
that don't fall within my property lines, and give me strength
to stand strong in those convictions. Build up the relationships
that encourage me and remind me who you made me to be.
Ultimately, draw my heart to authentic truth and love.

Think

My heart experiences greater freedom when I ask God to help
me discern where my physical, mental, emotional, and spiritual
"property lines" fall.

What Should I Allow into My Heart?

Finally, brothers and sisters, whatever is true,
whatever is noble, whatever is right, whatever is pure,
whatever is lovely, whatever is admirable—if anything
is excellent or praiseworthy—think about such things.

PHILIPPIANS 4:8

There's an experiment making the rounds on YouTube. A man's employer gives him the company credit card and permission to purchase everything advertised to him within a twenty-four-hour period. (Within reason, of course. The guy couldn't go out and buy a Ferrari even if he passed a Ferrari dealership!)

The day seemed to start innocently enough. The man saw an ad for coffee and allergy medication while he was watching the morning news, so he bought both of those things online. While on his way to work, he saw several items advertised in windows at various shops, and he purchased every single one of them. The billboards he passed became a shopping list for the afternoon. By the time he made it home at the end of the day, he'd purchased hundreds of items, some rather silly and some more practical, but all things he'd seen in an ad at some point throughout the day.

At the end of the video, the man sat surrounded by all his purchases, and suddenly the enormous volume of ads he'd been subjected to in a single day became glaringly apparent.

Most of us probably don't stop to consider the number of

messages we're taking in every day. Most of the time we're pretty good at filtering out the things we don't really need or care about.

But it's not always easy when someone says something that reaches straight into the deepest places of our hearts. It doesn't take much, either. One careless comment from somebody who doesn't know we're within hearing distance or a pointed remark from an acquaintance might be all it takes to knock us off our emotional feet, sometimes for a long while.

When we listen to and carry around everything we're told, especially in regard to who others think we are and who they think we should be, it can be like that guy buying all the stuff. Except we aren't just doing this for one day. It can be our whole lives! And carrying around all that stuff gets exhausting.

How do we combat that exhaustion? Is it even possible to sort through all the different messages we take in every day?

It is possible, of course, but it's not something that just . . . happens. Mold on an old loaf of bread stuffed in the back of the pantry just happens if we do nothing. An inch-deep layer of dust on top of our dressers just happens if we do nothing.

But a heart that doesn't hold on to bad messages and lies doesn't just happen. We have to do something, we have to take action. Otherwise, we do end up listening to and embracing things that aren't true about ourselves simply because someone said so.

We, alongside the guidance of God's Holy Spirit, are tasked with being the gatekeepers of our own hearts. Just like we can't always choose which advertisements show up on our way to school or work, we can't choose what others may say to or about us. But those messages don't have to hold any power over us. We choose what we take in and internalize.

A lot of lies exist about who we need to be and what we need to have in order to be happy. Some people will tell us if we run hard after success or money or a fairy-tale love story, we'll be fulfilled. We're often told we need more and deserve more to be happy. Then, seconds later, we're told we need to be less of ourselves if we want to fit in or if we want to matter to anyone else. These are lies, and we cannot expect them to bring life to our hearts.

Just like running water through a filter so it's safe to drink, we have to run the influences in our lives through a filter before they're safe for our hearts. For us, that filter is Philippians 4:8: "Finally, brothers and sisters, whatever is true, whatever is noble, whatever is right, whatever is pure, whatever is lovely, whatever is admirable—if anything is excellent or praiseworthy—think about such things."

So when you hear something, ask: Is the message we're taking in true? Is it noble, right, and pure? Is it lovely or admirable or excellent or praiseworthy?

Our hearts know. If we're looking a lie in the face—like if someone has told us God will never forgive us for what we've done, or if we're being told a certain experience will bring us ultimate fulfillment—then it doesn't have very far to filter before we toss it out. A lie, by its very definition, is the opposite of truth.

What if it *is* true, though? What if it passes through the first layer of the Philippians 4:8 filter? Maybe someone's said something that cuts deeply through to your soul because you know the things they've said are true, and it grieves you because you wish it wasn't your reality.

Then we keep passing it through the filters. The messages that pass through all the stages of the Philippians 4:8 filter are the ones we should truly believe.

This is a good way for us to evaluate all the people we choose to listen to and allow to speak into our lives. We'll never find a perfect friend here on earth. Even the best of friends will sometimes step on our toes or pinch our pride. But over time, we certainly find out exactly who belongs in our closest circle of friends. When we've chosen our friends carefully, we can be confident the messages they're speaking over and into us have some merit.

Truth is worth listening to. Jesus is worth listening to. The rest of it needs to be let go.

Live

What's a message you've been holding on to that doesn't pass through the Philippians 4:8 filter? Have you believed that message for so long that it almost seems true? Ask God to reveal the lies you've been believing about yourself, about your relationships, and about God himself.

To start filtering through the everyday messages that hit your heart in real time, memorize Philippians 4:8; and when you encounter a confusing situation or even a twinge from a real friend, see how that message measures up.

Pray

Holy Spirit, help me sort through all the messages I hear today. My heart sometimes feels crowded with the things I see and the messages I let inside. Sift through the lies and empower me to toss them away. Make the truth bright. Remind me of who I am, and help me remember that fact, especially when I start to believe lies.

Think

My heart is able to know that what God says about me is true, and I can immediately toss everything else.

What Do I Do with My Hurting Heart?

The LORD is close to the brokenhearted and saves those who are crushed in spirit.

PSALM 34:18

Your hurting heart is important.

It doesn't matter if the circumstances that caused your pain happened years ago or if something happened last night that sent your heart into a sadness spiral. Maybe you can pinpoint one event that knocked the air from your lungs and the joy from your soul like an exploding water balloon. Or maybe it's been more of a slow leak this time, and you're just now noticing your heart isn't nearly as light as it used to be.

Hurting hearts are not always an indicator that we've failed to guard them well enough. Pain is an indicator that something happened, and we need to slow down, step back, and pay attention.

If you accidentally slam your hand in a door, it *hurts*. Suddenly, you can feel your heartbeat in your fingertips. You cradle your hand and keep it close to your body to prevent further injury. Your fingers may turn nasty colors and start to swell up, depending on how bad the injury is. You may even need to visit a professional to discuss options to heal the damage.

If you ignore the pain and continue with life after your injury, gritting your teeth and pretending like nothing ever happened, you run the risk of making things worse.

Pain is a reality of life, not a cause for shame. Being sad or grieving a loss is a normal and healthy reaction when something happens that goes against what we'd expected or hoped for. Ignoring our hurting, tender hearts or trying to suck it up and get over it may seem like it helps for a little while, but broken things need a chance to heal well. Broken fingers that aren't dealt with will set incorrectly, and they lose the ability to do what they were meant to do over time because the pain wasn't taken care of at the beginning.

Psalm 34:18 says, "The LORD is close to the brokenhearted and saves those who are crushed in spirit." It doesn't say he looks down on the brokenhearted, angry with them for not being able to get it together. There's no mention of God shaking his head and saying, "I wish she'd pick herself up and move on already." Instead, he is close by. He saves us from feeling crushed inside. He will never leave us, no matter how hurt or broken we may feel.

Have you ever read the story of Hagar in the Bible? (If you haven't, pause for a minute and read through it. You can find an account of her broken heart in Genesis 16.) Hagar was an Egyptian slave under Hebrew rule in Abram and Sarai's household. Sarai, in an attempt to manage her own brokenness and confusion over her childlessness, tried to control the situation by giving Hagar to her husband so they could have children together.

Instead of ushering in healing, this brought chaos into their lives. When Hagar got pregnant (as Sarai had assumed would happen, since that was sort of her plan all along), Sarai became jealous and treated Hagar so terribly that Hagar felt her best option was to run away, heading to the desert to die.

Broken hearts that aren't acknowledged and cared for develop patterns for dealing with pain that aren't healthy. The longer those unhealthy patterns go unchecked, the more difficult it becomes to ever remember that wholeness and healing are an option. We become used to doing things a certain way to compensate for the pain. But lingering in a state of injury leads to long-term damage.

Not only do our hurting hearts cause immense pain for ourselves, they cause damage to other people in our lives as well if we've let our injuries fester. If you've ever encountered a hurting dog before, you know it can be dangerous to get close to them while they're in pain. Hurting animals snap and bite; hurting people have a tendency to do the same.

When Hagar got to the desert, she paused by a spring, and that's where the angel of the Lord found her. He found *her*. That means he knew she wasn't where she was meant to be, and he sought her out. God met her in the middle of her pain and confusion, and he had a conversation with her. He acknowledged her situation and her pain. In response, she named the place where they'd spoken "Beer Lahai Roi," or "well of the Living One who sees me." Hagar also gave God a name: The One who sees me.

That name still stands true today. God never changes, and he is to you what he was for Hagar. He is a God who sees your pain, and he willingly seeks you out when you're hurting.

However, he is also a God who heals, repairs, and restores. Though pain is a reality in this world, be encouraged because our God makes beautiful things out of ashes. It's who he is, and who he is doesn't change even when our circumstances waver.

Live

Think about a difficult situation you've been through. Whether it was years ago or this morning, reflect on where you are in your healing journey in regard to that situation. Have you taken the time to grieve your failed expectations? Have you spoken honestly with God about it? Is there anything you need to do right now to pursue healing?

Be truthful with yourself, unashamed of the sore spots in your heart. Ask God to guide you as you work through the hurt, and pray for him to lead you toward health and wholeness.

Pray

Holy Spirit, thank you for being with me even when my heart is hurting and angry. Thank you that I can be honest with you about how I feel, and that you understand and empathize. Even though I'm upset right now, I want to be careful not to linger in this hurting place. I want to pursue healing. Help me to remain softhearted. Help me avoid bitterness. Help me seek you when I'm discouraged. You are the God who sees. Thank you for seeing me right now.

Think

My heart begins to heal when I choose to deal with the hurt instead of hiding it or pretending it doesn't exist.

How to Cultivate a Joyful Heart

A cheerful heart is good medicine, but a crushed spirit dries up the bones.

PROVERBS 17:22

Strep throat is the worst. It makes your throat feel like it's engulfed in flames. Your tonsils feel like golf balls covered in thumbtacks. And you never want to drink anything ever again. Like, ever.

But if you go to the doctor and get an antibiotic to take care of those nasty white spots in the back of your throat, and if (*big if*) you can manage to choke down your antibiotics, most of the time the disease that caused such agony is gone by the time you wake up the next day. It's a miracle! You can eat and drink and be merry again without wondering if those activities will make you weep.

Having a crushed spirit sometimes feels similar to slogging through strep throat. There are points in our lives we experience such difficult times that our bones literally feel painful and ache simply because of the sadness in our hearts and not due to any disease.

Unfortunately, we can't go to a doctor to request a fast-acting, twenty-four-hour antibiotic for crushed spirits. If you do feel like the weight of your crushed spirit is too heavy to handle, talk to your doctor, therapist, or counselor. They won't be able to hand you a quick cure, but they will be able to help you. We can also, on our own, look for ways to restore our cheerful heart, the kind of cures Proverbs says are good medicine.

Cheerful hearts thrive when we serve others. This must be something God built into us at the very beginning, back when he created Adam and Eve to love and serve each other. When we serve, it reorients our hearts, reminding us of the things that really matter. It's easy to get caught up thinking we can't serve because we're too broke, too busy, or even too broken, but none of those things are true.

Serving others may require us to step outside of ourselves and our situations for a time, but that's not a bad thing. It isn't an easy thing either. So no scolding yourself when you don't feel like it or if you find the experience of helping others to be more difficult than you thought it would be. Just because something's hard doesn't mean you shouldn't do it. Ask God for the strength to step into the lives of others to bring extra joy to their days.

If you have a naturally cheerful heart, that's awesome! What a gift that is, to you and to those around you. Take that gift and use it to bring joy to others who need to know joy still exists. Not only will it strengthen your own heart, it will also bring light to those experiencing darkness. Let your cheerful heart be a soothing balm of Jesus' love in their lives.

Cheerful hearts also thrive when we set aside unrealistic expectations. Have you ever felt trapped under the weight of someone else's unrealistic expectation? Maybe a teacher expected you to be just like an older sibling, and you aren't. Perhaps a parent expected you to follow in their footsteps, to be passionate about the same sports or subjects, but as you get older you're starting to discover other things make your heart feel more alive.

When we don't live out someone else's unrealistic expectations for us, they often become disappointed, and that hurts. The truth is, carrying around another person's disappointment isn't on us. Those hang-ups and insecurities belong to them. Remember the boundaries we place around our hearts to guard them? Even so, others' reactions can still be painful. And what can feel even more painful and disappointing is when we place unrealistic expectations on ourselves.

Cheerful hearts can't thrive in an environment of unrealistic expectations—yours or anybody else's—so give yourself the gift of setting those expectations aside. Love those around you for who God made them to be, and love yourself for the same reason. So much freedom comes from enjoying life without demanding unreasonable feelings or actions from others or ourselves.

Cheerful hearts also thrive when we know and embrace our identities as women after God's heart. We've been created with a purpose. Our lives are not mistakes. We are needed and valued on this earth, and God gave us our personalities and our passions for a reason.

Accepting and believing labels other people put on us instead of believing God's words about who we are is a fast track toward a crushed and hurting spirit. Whatever people say to us and about us can be influenced by so many things: their negative experiences, their own hurting hearts and crushed spirits, their mood on that particular day, their relationship status. The only identity statements we need to lean into and accept as true are the ones God makes about us. All the rest can be weighed against what he says, and if they don't measure up, we get rid of them.

Notice what we haven't said here: cheerful hearts aren't always sickeningly sweet. They don't always *feel* happy. They aren't peppy to the point of being inauthentic. Sometimes being cheerful can mean allowing a loved one to be sad and sitting beside them to remind them they aren't alone, offering them something to hold on to during their difficulty.

Our authentically cheerful hearts have the power to change the world. We have the medicine sick hearts need. When we share it with everyone else, our joy increases even more.

Live

Is there something keeping you from living with a cheerful heart? Or does it feel more like you have a crushed spirit right now? It's likely we'll experience both in our lives.

Are the things you're doing building up a cheerful heart, or are you doing more to perpetuate a crushed spirit? Pick two or three things you can do this week to infuse your heart with a healthy dose of cheer.

Pray

Dear Jesus, my heart may not always feel cheerful, but I'd like to grow toward a joyful mindset because I want others to be able to recognize you. Help me keep my eyes open for ways that I can grow a more cheerful heart. Please also help me see patterns I'm stuck in that perpetuate a crushed spirit.

Think

My cheerful heart can be medicine to the world, drawing people in and showing them the love of Christ.

The Desires of My Heart

Take delight in the LORD, and he will give you the desires of your heart.

PSALM 37:4

What are the desires of your heart?

Are they material, like a few thousand dollars, a car that doesn't break down as often, or a shopping spree at your favorite boutique? Or are your desires things you can't hold, like a relationship with a guy you've been admiring from afar or a better relationship with your parents?

We wish for things that will add something special or exciting to our lives. Our hearts long to feel whole, and sometimes we think we'll reach a place where we have all the things we long for. Every time we see other people enjoying the things we crave, it magnifies the gap between what we have and what we want, and our hearts hurt. We want the space we're reserving for the things we desire to be filled.

When we read the words of Psalm 37:4, it's easy for our hearts to leap toward the hope and expectation of receiving those things *if* we only follow the instructions. "Take delight in the LORD," it says, "and he will give you the desires of your heart."

If we're not careful, we begin to treat those words like they're a formula for fulfillment.

We tell ourselves that reading the Bible, plus praying and going to church, plus desiring godly things equals all our desires coming to fruition. *If we do the right things*, we begin thinking, *God will reward us with what we want.*

But this verse isn't a formula to follow so we can be sure to receive the things we want. This is a promise for God's presence.

That doesn't mean we're going to be denied the things we've wished for. After all, God does take great delight in giving us gifts we don't deserve! We're absolutely free to enjoy the gifts he gives, thanking him for his provision of these things. But the gifts we receive that satisfy earthly desires will only bring partial fulfillment.

Possessions break. No relationship will be perfect.

But God! Only he can provide for us all we truly need—the real desires of our hearts. While we may lose things that we wished for or relationships we hoped to build, we cannot lose God's love for us.

This is a promise he's given us in Scripture. Romans 8:38–39 says, "For I am convinced that neither death nor life, neither angels nor demons, neither the present nor the future, nor any powers, neither height nor depth, nor anything else in all creation, will be able to separate us from the love of God that is in Christ Jesus our Lord."

When we run into difficulty, trauma, and other terribly painful things in life, getting the things we want may be able to numb the pain or take the edge off at times. But they are only temporary. They'll never be able to be our foundations when our hearts are hurting. But if we've built our trust upon the Lord, we will remain secure and steady regardless of life's difficulties.

When we "delight ourselves" with things we can see and experience, we enjoy those things only for the short time we see and experience them. And there's nothing wrong with enjoying those experiences. They may add wonderful flavor and nuance to our lives. But when we "delight ourselves" with the Lord, he doesn't just give us wonderful things. He *is* wonderful. And the things we experience when we draw closer to God last a lifetime.

We get to experience him in a deeper way when we seek his heart and when we get to know him more intimately for who he is, not for who we wish he would be. We spend time in his Word. We pray. We engage with other believers. We invite God into every single aspect of our lives, carrying on an ongoing conversation with him and keeping a watchful eye out for all the ways he's meeting us where we are. We use the unique talents and passions he's given us every day, and in doing so we can daily experience his nearness, because we are living the life he designed us to have.

God delights in you. His desire is for you to delight in him so you can experience a life full of his goodness right now.

Live

What are three things you can do today to delight yourself in the Lord? What are some areas in your life where you can be more aware of what God is doing and how he's at work? Are there any desires of your heart that you haven't talked to God about? Ask him. Wait for his answer.

Pray

Lord, I want to take the greatest delight in my relationship with you. I look forward to embracing and sharing the gifts you have given me. Please help me recognize all the ways you also meet me in my times of need. You are so much greater than anything I can think to ask for, and I love you.

Think

My heart is fulfilled only when I make an effort to experience God and live my life as a journey with him.

Using My Gifts to Glorify My Gift-Giver

Every good and perfect gift is from above, coming down from the Father of the heavenly lights, who does not change like shifting shadows.

JAMES 1:17

Imagine it's your birthday today (or maybe it is your birthday today . . . in which case, happy birthday!). So much cake! So much ice cream! Just enough confetti to make everything feel extra festive, but not enough to clog up the vacuum cleaner.

This year, your best friend *really* outdid herself with her present to you. It's something you never would have thought to ask for, but it so resonates with your heart in a way that makes you feel known, loved, and understood.

Now, let's imagine that a couple of months later, the gift is still every bit as wonderful as it was the day you unwrapped it, but the gift-giver isn't part of your life as much anymore. You think about, dream about, and enjoy the gift more than the best friend who gave it to you, even though she still loves you and cares for you just as much now as she did on the day she gave you the gift.

Looking at things from this perspective, it's easy to feel mortified. How could we forget that the gift we love so much wouldn't exist without the generosity and love of the gift-giver?

But this is how we sometimes treat God. James 1:17 says God gives us "every good and perfect gift." Our talents and our passions are gifts in our lives from our God who cares for us. The good things God gives us are ways for us to enjoy life in his presence. But when we elevate those gifts over him, we corrupt the gifts and become slaves to them instead.

People don't start out with addictions—there's always a journey that takes us closer to the things that tangle around our hearts. It's entirely possible for us to become bent on serving our passions instead of serving the one who gave us our passions. When we notice ourselves serving our dreams instead of serving our Lord, it's time to step back and remember the purpose of our gifts.

The purpose of our gifts is to help us know the ultimate Gift-Giver. God didn't randomly distribute our talents and our passions. He gave those things to us because *he knew* how they would make us feel, what those things would awake in us, and how those things would remind us of how much he loves us.

The gifts God gives to each of us are incredibly diverse. None of us are gifted with exactly the same things in exactly the same ways. They reflect the creativity, care, and knowledge of our divine Gift-Giver.

The purpose of our gifts is to lead us farther into an enjoyable relationship with our Gift-Giver. Have you ever thought of your gifts as a method of worship? They can be! Since God's the one who gave us our gifts in the first place, isn't it reasonable to think that he gave us the desire to use them so we could enjoy his presence more because of them? If you're a creative person, enjoy your creativity and ask God to meet you there. If you love nature, spend time outside and keep watch for the ways God will show up. If business and numbers are more your thing, go all in! God is pleased to do that work beside you. Watch for all the ways God nudges your heart as you lean into your talents and strengths, glorifying him in the process.

The purpose of our gifts is to give us a way to share our Gift-Giver with the rest of the world. Our talents and gifts haven't been given to us so we can hoard them and keep them hidden from others. Use them to show the people in your life how wonderful our Gift-Giver is. Bless others unconditionally out of the abundance of your gifts and show them how they are equally loved and gifted by our Creator as well.

Live

In what ways do you think you've been uniquely gifted by God? What gifts, talents, and passions do you have that resonate with the purpose you believe God has given you? How will you worship God as you embrace your gifts? Examine your heart and ask God to reveal if you sometimes treat the gifts he has given you as though they are more important than your relationship with him.

Pray

Dear God, thank you for the unique gifts, talents, and passions you've given me. I'm grateful for the unique ways you've put me together—body, mind, heart, and spirit. If I'm more dedicated to making my personal dreams come true than I am dedicated to you, please show that to me and give me the courage to turn away from that behavior. I want to enjoy the gifts you've given me, and I'm excited to know you better because of them.

Think

My heart will flourish and thrive when I enjoy my relationship with God, embracing the gifts and talents he's given me and letting them teach me more about his heart.

When We're Tired of Waiting

I remain confident of this: I will see the goodness of the LORD in the land of the living. Wait for the LORD; be strong and take heart and wait for the LORD.

PSALM 27:13-14

There's not a single person on earth who hasn't waited on something. We wait at red lights. We wait for our food at restaurants. We wait for grades to be posted.

Have you ever made those paper chains, the ones where you tear a loop off with every day that passes to count down to a long-awaited event? That works well when we know the day our waiting will be over, like looking forward to the end of school or the beginning of summer camp. But what about when we aren't sure if the waiting will *ever* end?

We all have dreams and longings stored up in our hearts. As much as we long for something, though, we can't be sure those things will ever happen for us, even if we think about, hope for, and wish for them every day. We start out feeling strong. "Yeah," we say to ourselves after forty-eight hours, "I can wait. I'll keep praying about this, and God will answer. It's fine."

But then weeks pass. The boy decides to date somebody else, or the friends forget their promise, or the doctors can't figure out the problem. When the circumstances worsen, our faith might start to waiver. And when weeks turn to months, and those months turn to years, our hearts might feel like they're breaking.

Where is God in the waiting? Does he even care about the things we so desperately wish for? And, though it's scary and defeating to think about, what happens if the things we're waiting for never happen? Is God's presence in our lives enough?

If we're really honest with ourselves, sometimes the answer to that question is no. It doesn't always feel like God's presence is enough to fill the void left by the thing we are waiting on. Sometimes, instead, it feels like our hearts will surely wither up and crumble if we have to wait even one more second for our dreams to be fulfilled. Or it seems like we've been abandoned, forgotten, and left behind.

Those feelings make complete sense. Though we may love Jesus with all our hearts, life is still a big struggle at times. Our negative feelings aren't necessarily *bad,* though they don't always tell us the truth of the situation. In fact, Jeremiah 17:9 even goes so far as to say, "The heart is deceitful above all things and beyond cure."

Times of waiting are like fertile ground. We can choose what we'd like to grow in that space. If we let our feelings become the most important driver of our lives while we wait, we can sow seeds of anger, hostility, and bitterness. We can buy into the idea that we've been abandoned by God, that he doesn't care about the things that are important to us.

When we believe God isn't meeting our needs and easing our pain because he doesn't care, it's easy to let those abandonment feelings and thoughts take root and grow. Sometimes it seems like they become our heart's default, even if we've been followers of Jesus for a long time. Because we can't readily see God's faithfulness, we doubt it even exists—because we can't envision any possible way for him to make things right.

An alternate—and admittedly harder—way to tackle the difficulties of waiting is to create a mindset contrary to the way we feel by trusting the Lord even in the hard times of waiting in our lives. We can sew seeds of hope, trust, and patience. This is part of what it looks like to have faith.

Psalm 27:14 says to "be strong" as we wait for the Lord. Being strong takes hard work, doesn't it? We can't show up to the gym with wimpy noodle arms and start doing bicep curls with the thirty-pound dumbbells. We'll probably have to start out with those four-pound dumbbells instead and do a lot of work and training over a long period of time. We won't always feel like training, and sometimes we'll put the weights down in favor of relaxing.

In our times of waiting, however, we don't have the luxury of lowering the weights. We can't take a break when we're tired or step away from the situations that cause us trouble. But the good news is *God* is strong, and he is *our* strength (Psalm 28:7 says so!). We don't need to train in order to receive his strength—he offers it to us because he is infinitely good and kind to us—but we do need to exercise our trust in him often so it's easier to lift the emotional weights in our lives and hand them over to him.

In the dreary, difficult days of waiting, we have to make the decision to trust God with the present and the future. He's been faithful in the past and has proven himself. Even if we have trouble remembering the specifics from our own lives, we can read the stories of his faithfulness to others in the Bible to remind ourselves of the truth of God's character.

As the Alpha and Omega (Greek letters that mean *beginning* and *end*), God sees everything through the lens of the fullness of time, and there's nothing that escapes his perception. Though we don't know when the ending will come to our waiting—whether it will rush in like a tidal wave or gently dissipate like the recession of fog in the morning—our God knows. He cares about how our hearts will fare during our waiting, and he sees the greater purpose and strength we'll gain in these times.

Even though our waiting isn't predictable, God is good, and he can be trusted to meet us in the middle of the waiting, and remain faithful and loving through it. God will not let our waiting go to waste.

Live

What are you waiting on? Does it feel like you're going to be waiting forever? How does your heart feel as you wait? Are there deeper issues your feelings point toward? Today, remind yourself of all the ways God has been faithful to you and to everyone who's come before you, in order to shore yourself up and remind you to trust, even in uncertainty.

Pray

Dear Lord, I get seriously tired of waiting. The things I'm waiting for are so important to me. I wish I could say I believe your presence is enough for me, but sometimes I don't feel like that's true. Please breathe truth into my heart. Help me remember your faithfulness even when things seem impossible or the wait feels endless.

Think

My heart can trust that God will not let my waiting be wasted, even when my feelings may say otherwise.

When My Heart Is Afraid

"Be strong and courageous. Do not be afraid or terrified because of them, for the Lord your God goes with you; he will never leave you nor forsake you."

DEUTERONOMY 31:6

In science class, it's common to see a bunch of furry, spotted petri dishes sitting out on the lab counters, especially around science fair season. There's usually at least one kid who does that terrifying (and effective) experiment about household surfaces and the bacteria harbored there. After swabbing toilet seats, sponges, and cell phones, the science fair competitor touches the swabs to petri dishes prepped with agar, a gel particularly friendly to bacteria. Agar doesn't break down when the bacteria start to grow—instead, it allows us to see exactly what sort of insidious things are growing all over our homes.

Agar is to bacteria what uncertainty can be to fear. We feel pretty good when things are solid and we're reasonably sure of what's coming up ahead. But when life goes wild, as it has a tendency to do, and we start to look at things in a new way, fear makes the situation more colorful, intense, and harder to handle.

Can you relate to this? Has your heart ever felt completely overwhelmed with feelings of fear, to the point you feel paralyzed?

Joshua might have felt that way when he found out he was going to take over soon and be the one to lead Israel into the promised land (which happened to be filled with giants . . . something the Israelites weren't expecting). But Moses presented Joshua to the entire lot of rowdy Israelites and told him, "Be strong and courageous, for you must go with this people into the land that the LORD swore to their ancestors to give them . . . The LORD himself goes before you and will be with you; he will never leave you nor forsake you. Do not be afraid; do not be discouraged" (Deuteronomy 31:7–8). If Joshua weren't feeling fearful and weak, would God have needed to tell him these words through Moses?

Sometimes we might read these verses as a statement of disappointment, sort of like, "Wow, Joshua. Get it together. Quit being afraid already." And when we read this and the other "do not fears" listed in the Bible (there are quite a few of them), we might automatically feel like God's disappointed in us. We can't seem to get it together long enough to kick fear to the curb.

But God doesn't tell us to not be afraid as an angry admonishment. Out of his heart of empathy, he's reminding us we don't have to be afraid because he will never forsake us.

When kids are scared, good parents don't scold them for feeling afraid. Those parents are compassionate to what their children are feeling because they know the bigger picture isn't all that scary. For example, when their kid is afraid of what lurks underneath the bed, their perspective allows them to know their kids don't *need* to be afraid, but there's no reason to be angry at the child because of the fear.

God knows everything about of our entire lives and all our experiences. See how he reminds Joshua that he will never leave or forsake him? We can be sure this promise applies to us too. God doesn't change, and his character stays the same. He won't leave or forsake us either.

When God says to be strong and courageous, it's a reminder to us that fear isn't the fullness of our story. There's still a bigger picture, and he's there in the middle of it.

Not only does God know the full picture of our entire lives, he understands why we're afraid, and he can see why we don't *need* to be afraid. He's already overcome everything we're afraid of, and he's more powerful than all these things. John 16:33 says, "In me you may have peace. In this world you will have trouble. But take heart! I have overcome the world."

God is aware of our enemies and he sees how our hearts are in a constant battle. He's not afraid. He is greater than anyone and everything that threatens us.

We will have trouble because we live in a fallen world where sin and fear run rampant. But fear isn't our destination. As God's children, we will share in his final victory over fear and sin. We don't need to work harder to control our fear when the trouble in the world feels overwhelming. And having peace doesn't mean we'll never struggle with fear. Peace isn't constant happy feelings. It's confidence in God's strength and in his victory. Peace happens when we trust God and choose to have faith that he is with us even in our darkest times of fear.

Of course, sometimes it still feels like fear is winning, like when we let fear convince us of untruths about God or about ourselves. Fear feels like it's winning when it causes us to lose perspective and forget victory is ahead. But even if we temporarily forget God is greater than all our fears, he's not to going to leave us there.

Each minute is another opportunity for new beginnings and another opportunity to remind ourselves who has already rescued us and where the true power lies. Just because fear took over one minute, that doesn't mean it has to take over the rest of them. While fear may whisper and sometimes shout to our hearts, it will never be victorious over our Savior.

Live

Are you afraid right now? How do you think God reacts when your heart feels sick with anxiety? Imagine God drawing you into his arms and cradling you close to himself, sheltering you from all the uncertainty and fear. Remember, he's compassionate toward you even when you're afraid.

Pray

Dear Lord, open my eyes so I can accurately see how you feel about me. Show me the ways you are active and strong in the situations I'm working through right now, in the places I feel weak. My heart is afraid more often than it is strong. I know you're greater than fear, and I need to experience that in my life right now. Give me your strength and your perspective so I can trust in your knowledge of the bigger picture and in your unending care for me.

Think

My heart can be sure that God is who he says he is and that he cares deeply for me, and my fear doesn't change who he is or how he feels about me.

Having a Heart of Integrity

But the fruit of the Spirit is love, joy, peace,
forbearance, kindness, goodness, faithfulness,
gentleness and self-control. Against such things
there is no law. Those who belong to Christ Jesus
have crucified the flesh with its passions and desires.
Since we live by the Spirit, let us keep in step with
the Spirit.

GALATIANS 5:22–25

If we go to an apple orchard, we expect to pick apples. If we walk up to an apple tree with a basket and all we find growing on the apple tree are peaches, we'd have a lot of questions. Starting with, "Why in the world is this apple tree growing a bunch of peaches?"

Apple trees produce apples and peach trees produce peaches. We even look to the fruit to help us identify the tree. It's obvious that an apple tree is what it is because it's covered in apples.

People are the same way. When our hearts are in relationship with Jesus (meaning we spend time with Jesus and look to grow our connection with him), the "fruit" in our lives is good. These fruits are thoughts and behaviors like what Jesus had when he lived here on earth, and there's a succinct list in Galatians 5:22 for us to reference. Things like real love, joy, peace, patience (forbearance), kindness, goodness, faithfulness, and self-control are the fruits of a heart that loves God. When our lives are full of these qualities, nurtured by a healthy relationship with Jesus, people identify us as Christ followers by the "fruit" we produce. They don't question who we belong to because it's obvious from the way we live. The fruits of a heart in love with Jesus are good fruits.

The opposite is also true. The fruits of a heart in love with sin are rotten. In Matthew 7:15–18, Jesus warns us, "Watch out for false prophets. They come to you in sheep's clothing, but inwardly they are ferocious wolves. By their fruit you will recognize them." He goes on to say, "Every good tree bears good fruit, but a bad tree bears bad fruit. A good tree cannot bear bad fruit, and a bad tree cannot bear good fruit."

Whatever we nurture and tend in our hearts, whether it's good or rotten, will show itself in the way we live our lives.

Sometimes we may think we're different from everyone else, that the little sins we keep tucked away won't matter in the long run. We lie to ourselves, somehow convincing our hearts that secret, sinful behaviors only affect us. We might even get so good at lying to ourselves that we start believing our sinful behaviors don't even make a difference because we can manage our hearts just fine.

This isn't truth, and it's a sign of a heart lacking integrity. People often tell us that having integrity means doing the right thing even when nobody else is watching, and that's part of it. But another piece of integrity relates to our hearts.

Because when we feed secret sins, we have to split our hearts to make life work without blowing our cover. If we don't want our parents or friends to find out about a sinful habit, we have to behave differently around them than we do when we're engaging in that sin. We can't imagine having them around while we're indulging in that behavior. It's almost as though we must become different people to keep our sins a secret while we live the rest of our lives. After a while, the gap between the "parts" of us grows wider. Eventually, we won't be able to keep the gross parts of our heart hidden. The fruit of a sinful heart will show up no matter how hard we work to cover it up.

Proverbs 11:3 says, "The integrity of the upright guides them, but the unfaithful are destroyed by their duplicity." A duplicitous person is deceitful, and we often refer to them as being "double-minded." These are people who speak of themselves one way and act in another.

We shouldn't live as though we're several different people, managing many reputations and lifestyles for each friend group and situation. A person of integrity is free to be the same person with her church friends as she is with her school friends as she is with her family.

Instead of being rotten on the inside and split into many pieces, we want our hearts to be full of integrity and whole so the fruits others see when they spend time with us are those that point back to Jesus.

A heart of integrity thrives when we're vulnerable with safe people. The lies we buy into, the things we convince ourselves are okay when they're clearly wrong, and the stuff we do to mask deeper issues are all things that can lead to rotten fruit. But if we're brave and we talk about our struggles with trustworthy, godly people, then sin loses its power over us. There's a lot of good in being accountable to someone who won't judge your behavior but who will still remind you when you've gone off course.

Satan likes for things to stay secret because it's easier to convince ourselves there isn't a problem . . . until it's taken over and destroyed our lives. So find someone who will encourage you to leave the junk behind and pursue growth as the woman God intends for you to be. Once the struggles are dragged out into the open, they become much easier to fight, especially when we're reassured we aren't fighting alone.

A heart of integrity thrives when we apologize for and repent of (or stop participating in) the behaviors and beliefs that pull our hearts toward rottenness. It isn't a question of whether we're going to have rotten behaviors that pop up. We all have sinful patterns we'll have to learn to recognize and weed out throughout our whole lives. The difference between a heart of integrity and a heart of duplicity, though, is that a woman with a heart of integrity will quickly start fighting to get rid of the junk. She's honest about where she struggles and doesn't give up when she stumbles. She also doesn't revel in or celebrate the sin that produces rotten fruit.

Our hearts don't have to stay bound to the behaviors that produce rotten fruits. Jesus offers us restoration when we're in relationship with him, and that means our hearts too. If the things you've been doing in secret, or even out loud, produce destruction or deceit, turn away and start chopping them out of your life. A heart of integrity is worth the work now, and the benefits will reach far beyond today.

Live

What can you do today to jumpstart your dedication to having a heart of integrity? Where in your life do you recognize even the barest beginnings of duplicity? Is there someone you know who will allow you to be vulnerable about your struggles without shaming you for them?

Pray

Dear Lord, it's important to me that my heart is whole, and that means I need a heart of integrity. I want to dedicate myself to what's right in my spirit, so help me discern between right and wrong. When I sin and it has the potential to become a pattern, help me to recognize it quickly and make me brave enough to get rid of it entirely, immediately.

Think

I have a heart of integrity when I am authentic and aware of the "fruit" in my life, and whether that fruit represents my relationship with Christ well or not.

Breaking Free from a Heart of Legalism

But whatever were gains to me I now consider loss for the sake of Christ. What is more, I consider everything a loss because of the surpassing worth of knowing Christ Jesus my Lord, for whose sake I have lost all things. I consider them garbage, that I may gain Christ and be found in him, not having a righteousness of my own that comes from the law, but that which is through faith in Christ—the righteousness that comes from God on the basis of faith.

PHILIPPIANS 3:7–9

Many of us want to be a part of a club, whether it's a club made up of our best friends or something at school. We feel like we belong because we wear the same clothes as everyone else in the group or we sit at a specific table in the lunchroom together. When we're younger, we gather in clubhouses that require secret knocks or passwords before we can gain entrance. If you didn't know the knock or the password? Forget it. You weren't allowed.

Most clubs make it clear: only certain people with certain behaviors are allowed in.

Sometimes we do the same thing with faith in Jesus.

Only people who follow a certain code of ethics are allowed in. We might say we welcome everyone, but on Sunday mornings, when we see the gentleman with the tattooed face and shredded jeans, we feel extra proud of ourselves for going to a church that allows people "like that" through the doors. "Good Christians" are the ones who follow all the rules—all of *our* rules—and everybody else needs lots of improvement before we consider them to be fellow Jesus followers.

We get caught up in specifics like hemlines and jewelry, style and appearances. Faith becomes a journey of rule-following instead of one of relationship. We think we're living in freedom because we don't do certain things, when we've actually been lured into a gospel of legalism. But serving rules isn't freedom; serving Jesus is.

Instead of freedom, we're stuck in bondage to the shoulds and shouldn'ts. We can tell we're enslaved this way if we get angry with anyone who breaks the extrabiblical rules we've set up to supposedly keep us on the straight and narrow. Or we think one rule is good, so one hundred rules must be better, and anyone who breaks one of the hundred must be well off course. We make assumptions about the hearts of people who break our rules and become so convinced we're spiritually better that we forget to love. The truth is, though, we aren't better. Our hearts and theirs have the same exact starting point—separation from God.

Our long lists of Christian rules are an attempt to cover up something few of us are brave enough to admit: believing God will somehow like us more if we follow more rules. But extra rules don't equal extra credit in God's kingdom. We're not made right because of what we do or don't do. Philippians 3:8 says we have no righteousness of our own that comes through following the law, but only righteousness through faith in Jesus Christ.

Our inability to serve God without sinning goes all the way back to Adam and Eve in the garden of Eden. When we make what we do or don't do more important than what Jesus has already done, we're preaching a false gospel with our lives, one that says salvation all depends on us. It also leads to a heavy burden of rule following, one that none of us are strong enough to carry.

This doesn't draw people toward Jesus or toward us either. People who don't know Jesus will have a hard time believing us when we say, "God is love," when they're witnessing our lifestyles propped up by rules and regulations designed to keep us in right standing with the Lord. It is *his* free gift of grace that will help us make disciples, not our rules.

When we're enslaved to the rules, believing it's necessary to stay in the corner of our unlocked prison cells, our world becomes very small. Instead of doing the dangerous work of loving everyone else "out there" in the rest of the world, regardless of whether or not they follow the same rules we do, we keep hiding where we think it's safe. We guard our hearts in the wrong way, instead of opening them up to those who need to hear and see God's love in action.

There's another way the pendulum can swing—when we do everything we want, whenever we want, however we want, rebelling against all rules and wisdom. Here we become enslaved to sins that put our feel-good experiences on a pedestal. Those things become the idols we worship when instead we should be worshiping Jesus.

Sin is still sin. There is no freedom in it. It isn't life-giving, and it doesn't lead us closer to Jesus. Throwing out all boundaries will lead to destruction, and we absolutely must turn away from legitimate sin in our lives.

Freedom doesn't come to us through sinning more, and we also can't sock away extra freedom by following more rules. The only way we'll experience true liberty is if we're loving God, seeking him with all our hearts, and following *his* commands. Everything else is worth letting go.

Live

Reflect on the way you live your life, not the way you would like to live or on the things you say because you feel like you're supposed to say them. And be honest with yourself. Are there rules you've made up because you want extra credit from God? Or are there sin patterns you need to kick to the curb? Think about ways you may be enslaved, then ask God to help you move toward freedom instead.

Pray

Dear Jesus, give me wisdom. I want to live a life that's pleasing to you. I don't want to get so hung up on following made-up rules that I fail to remember the glory and goodness of what you've already done for me. Help me to love you and love others with all my heart, and remind me when I may be getting overly attached to the shoulds and shouldn'ts I've imposed on myself. I want to be free to love you, to love myself, and to love others.

Think

My heart is free because I know and love Jesus, not because I follow a specific set of rules.

Tuning My Heart to God's

Submit yourselves, then, to God. Resist the devil, and he will flee from you. Come near to God and he will come near to you. Wash your hands, you sinners, and purify your hearts, you double-minded.

JAMES 4:7–8

*D*o you play an instrument like the guitar, trumpet, or cello? If you do, you know how important it is to keep your instrument tuned up. Music played on an instrument that isn't in tune sounds discordant. Even if we don't have an expert ear, when an instrument isn't in tune, it's not as lovely as it could be because the instrument hasn't been adjusted to match the right standard.

Middle C is middle C whether we think it should be or not. We can say middle C should sound like any other note, but that's simply not true. And if we tune our instruments with that belief, we'll find that our instruments don't sound the way they are intended. Musicians use tools like tuning forks so they can hear the standard and know when an instrument has gone out of tune.

As we spend time with and listen to God, our hearts become more tuned to his. Just like with our instruments, we can't steep our hearts in whatever sounds good to us, because he has a standard of truth. We have to tune our hearts to the Expert's ear.

James says that if we come near to God, he will come near to us. It's a promise, and we can trust it. But that's easier said than done sometimes. How can we connect with the God of the universe? We can't just buy him a latte or go to lunch with him and ask all the questions on our minds.

The rest of the Bible has lots of suggestions for connecting with God. Read about the life of Jesus if you want to see the *best* example for connecting with our Father. Here are a few ideas to get you started right now.

Draw near to God through reading Scripture. If we want to tune our hearts to truth, we can't ignore God's Word. No other book contains more of God's heart. Maybe you've heard someone refer to the Bible as God's love letter to us, and that makes a lot of sense because it's the whole, comprehensive story of God's pursuit of our hearts. There are a lot of great books that elaborate on concepts from the Bible or break them out thematically and teach us how to look at them more critically, and there's nothing wrong with those books. But if we really want to settle in and be near to God's heart, there's no substitute for reading his Word.

Draw near to God's heart through prayer. Prayer is speaking to God, voicing our gratitude and our concerns, and then being still and aware in his presence. It takes courage to sit with God in prayer, to set aside all the distractions from our day and our racing thoughts, and to be quiet and mindful. It's hard not to be distracted. Sometimes it can help to write down our prayers or to read guided prayers. However we choose to connect with God through prayer, we can be sure it helps refocus our hearts back on him.

Draw near to God's heart through confession and repentance. Sin isn't fun to talk about, but it's one thing every single one of us here on earth has in common. It's why we need Jesus, and it will continue to drive a wedge between us and God if we let it. But if we face our sin head-on, confess, and repent, we rest in forgiveness instead of steeping in filth.

Draw near to God through endurance. Nobody has to work hard to convince us life isn't always easy. Your story could very well be one of a lot of pain, more than many of your peers or even more than many adults. The news hasn't been very positive since . . . well, since the fall way back in Genesis. We live in a broken world, and things get really messed up sometimes.

But for us as Christ followers, the difficulties we face are opportunities to lean into God's heart, to trust him even when nothing makes sense, and to believe God is who he says he is. We know all will be made right one day because God has promised it to us. In the meantime, we wait. We persevere. We endure. Romans 5:3–4 says, "We know that suffering produces perseverance; perseverance, character; and character, hope." We can be women of hope in every circumstance—the wonderful and the awful alike—because we trust God and believe what he's told us.

God is not at all afraid of our hurting hearts, whether we've brought our pain on ourselves or it's a product of something that's happened to us. He promises to be with us in *all* things, and we can trust him.

Draw near to God's heart through community. Our lives aren't only about us. We live on earth with over seven billion people right now. Even with that kind of number, it's entirely likely we sometimes feel alone or cut off from the rest of the world. Yes, it's true that God is a Father to the fatherless and he is always with us, but he's also given us the opportunity to be a part of various communities.

When we live in community with other Christ followers, we get to hear about and experience God's faithfulness in their lives. Our faith is strengthened when we witness the ways God provides for our friends in times of trouble. These communities are where we get to rejoice in who God is with people who also know him. Christian communities should be places where we can safely learn how to love, how to forgive, how to rejoice, and how to grieve, all with people who are learning the same things.

We can also be in community with others who aren't like us, and this teaches us how to love even when it feels uncomfortable. It's easy to love the lovable or to love people who act like us. But when people come from a different culture or when they simply do things differently than we might, we're tempted to go the other direction out of fear or discomfort.

God can, and will, meet us when we reach out to others whether they have a lot in common with us or nothing at all. Jesus spent a lot of time with people who weren't like him, such as tax collectors and Pharisees and prostitutes, and he welcomed them into his community. Because Jesus chose to reach out to others, drawing them into his life and experiences, these people were able to see God's heart firsthand. Hopefully, others who engage with us will be able to say one day that they also see the Holy Spirit in us.

All of these things are simply ideas of ways we can draw nearer to God's heart. But these things aren't things we do to make God happier with us (though he *is* happy to draw near to us); these are things we do to meet God, to experience life with him, and to share his love with everyone else we meet.

Live

Where is your heart in need of a tune-up? How can you listen for God's heart and tune yours back to his today? Take fifteen minutes out of your day to seek his heart and to draw near to him, no matter what else is going on. Set aside all the distractions as best as you can and ask him to draw near to you.

Pray

God, you said if I draw near to you, you will draw near to me. I need your nearness in my life, and I trust you to do as you promised. Tune my heart to you and to your truth, and help me to recognize your nearness no matter the circumstance.

Think

My heart sometimes gets out of tune, but God reminds me his heart is my standard, and he helps me get back in tune when we spend time together.

My Heart's Companions

You will keep in perfect peace those whose minds are steadfast, because they trust in you. Trust in the LORD forever, for the LORD, the LORD himself, is the Rock eternal.

ISAIAH 26:3–4

In races like the Kentucky Derby, the horses running around the track are thoroughbreds. They're fast, high-energy athletes bred for a specific task. When they get to the track, they're buzzing with exhilaration. The energy from the grandstands only adds to the excitement. There's a reason why the gates open as quickly as possible after the last horse is in place. Jockeys don't want to be stuck in a small space on a high-strung racehorse. And who can blame them!

Everybody notices the thoroughbreds. But have you ever noticed the other horses at the racetrack—the stocky ones who seem like they're more likely to munch on the clover than sprint laps? They may not seem like much, but these horses, called lead ponies, are actually a big deal.

Lead ponies are the gentle, steady companions to the high-strung, easily distracted racehorses. When the thoroughbreds get stressed out, the lead ponies are there as a grounding presence. Lead ponies get gnawed on by anxious pals; they chase down runaways; they reassure their buddies on the track with comforting snorts and whinnies. Without the lead ponies, chaos reigns.

Whether we're aware of it or not, all of us have lead ponies in our lives. When we're feeling nervous and high-strung, we seek out a companion. We all run to something.

That may mean that when we run into rocky situations that make our stomachs churn, we run to our chosen escape companion and use it to pretend nothing is happening. We don't want to deal with the problem, so we're just gonna turn up the TV to drown out the noise. Or we seek out friends, who despite their best intentions can never fully give us the calm and peace we seek.

Or we may make the wise choice of turning to Christ as our companion. This is, without a doubt, the best choice. He's the only one who is always present and will stay alongside us in times of difficulty, gently nudging us and reminding us of his faithfulness and the hope we have in spite of our circumstances.

Aren't sure what lead ponies you're tied to? Take a look at what you're doing. Unravel those threads, the coping strategies you're employing, and work your way through until you reach the center of the knot. The things we engage in to heal the hurt or fill the void are just distractions from our true needs.

If we've tied ourselves to something destructive, we'll never find peace. We'll seek healing and wholeness from people or objects that have no power to give us those things.

Isaiah 26:3–4 says, "You will keep in perfect peace those whose minds are steadfast, because they trust in you. Trust in the LORD forever, for the LORD, the LORD himself, is the Rock eternal." Peace is absolutely possible, even in the most desperate, difficult situations we find ourselves in. But there is only one source.

Peace is a result of trust, not in what we can do or how we can handle the stuff we're working through, but in who God is and what he does. Throughout Scripture we're shown exactly who he is. When we read about how God's met and provided for others in the Bible, it reminds us how he still meets us and provides for us today.

When God tells us who he is, we can take him at his word. He named himself the "LORD who heals" when caring for the Israelites in the desert, and he is *still* the same healer today. When Gideon built an altar to God and called it "The LORD Is Peace," that statement stands true even now because God is the same God to us that he was to Gideon. He is the same God to us as he was to Moses and the Israelites. People are the ones who change, but God remains unchanging and trustworthy.

Because of who God is, we can have peace even in the middle of the feelings that make our stomachs ache and our hearts shatter. Peace that comes out of the trust we've placed in God isn't dependent on our feelings.

We can't steady ourselves. No matter how strong we believe ourselves to be, we'll never be able to handle everything we walk through in life by ourselves. We have to stay close to Jesus, the one who's steadier than we can ever be. Everyone and everything else will disappoint. Nobody else is able to love us 100 percent of the time. Nothing else will satisfy us 100 percent of the time.

God doesn't demand our trust—he invites us into it. Isaiah 26:3 is an offer to embrace what we cannot provide for ourselves.

But one thing to remember is that the peace that comes from God isn't the absence of uncomfortable feelings. Instead, it's confidence in the fact that God is aware of even the smallest details of our lives. It's remembering that God knows exactly how all the pieces of our story will integrate to tell his greater story. Peace is trusting that, even though our circumstances are gross or painful or dark, God is still who he says he is and that we have not been abandoned. And with that in mind, we can move beyond the fear and anxieties we feel—the lies that are trying to stir up our hearts and cause chaos—and embrace the reality that our Comforter has everything under control.

Live

Who or what are you leaning into in an effort to find peace? Have you gotten in the habit of running to things that bring about destruction and disappointment instead? How can you choose to trust in God's character and seek the peace he provides instead?

Pray

Dear Jesus, I'm not always good at seeking you first when I desperately need peace. It seems so much easier to run to things that I can touch and see than it is to come to you. I know there's nothing here on earth that can provide me with the peace I'm looking for. Everything else is a poor substitute for what you provide. I believe you are who you say you are. I trust you to remain steady even in the middle of my downright awful circumstances. You are trustworthy, and today I choose to trust you to provide the peace I need.

Think

My heart is peaceful when I trust not in my own power, but in the power of God and his love and faithfulness toward me.

PART TWO

God's Heart

Knowing God's Heart by Knowing His Names

Moses said to God, "Suppose I go to the
Israelites and say to them, 'The God of your
fathers has sent me to you,' and they ask me,
'What is his name?' Then what shall I tell them?"
God said to Moses, "I AM WHO I AM. This is what
you are to say to the Israelites: 'I AM has sent me
to you.'"

EXODUS 3:13–14

hen we first meet new people, we introduce ourselves
and tell them our names. If we're ever in a group setting where we don't know each other, we usually have
to wear nametags. Our names are often the first piece of information we tell people about ourselves. The beginning step to
knowing someone is knowing what they call themselves.

Do you know why you received your name? Maybe your
parents poured over baby name books and had a list, then chose
their favorite for you when they first laid eyes on your teeny, tiny
babyness. Or maybe a caregiver or a nanny at an orphanage or
foster home just knew you were meant to be a . . . your name.
A lot of people are given family names or honor names, chosen
for them to celebrate a relationship or the memory of a loved
one who has already passed away. And it's possible you even
acquired a nickname when you were younger that everyone now
uses instead of the name on your birth certificate!

In the Bible, names often mean something.

Jesus' name literally means "The LORD is salvation," a name God chose for his son long before he was born on earth.

Naomi, Ruth's mother-in-law, asked her friends to call her Mara after losing her whole family. She felt she could no longer relate to Naomi, which means "pleasant," and preferred to be called Mara, meaning "bitter," instead.

The well where the angel of the Lord met Hagar in Genesis 16 is called *Beer Lahai Roi*, a name which means "Well of the Living One who sees me."

Names in the Bible are a statement of identity; they're a clue as to what that place or person is all about.

God uses several names for himself throughout Scripture, and each one of those names points directly to an aspect of his heart and teaches us about his character. The names in Scripture may sound funny to us because many of them are awkward, long, and hard to pronounce. But our Bibles usually have footnotes to tell us what these names mean in our languages.

In the Bible, God is Jehovah-Raah, "the Lord who shepherds," and Jehovah-raphe, "the Lord who heals." He's Jehovah-Jireh, "the LORD will provide." He's also Jehovah-Shalom, "the LORD is peace."

And this is just a short list. These names point to God's care for each of us, his healing power, his ability to provide, and his peace. There are still other names throughout the Bible that speak of his eternal nature, his constant presence, his protection, and his holiness.

But these are just descriptive names—kind of like a teacher referring to you as "the go-getter of the team" because you're always out to make a great play on the field, or a friend calling you "the reliable one" because you're always there when she needs you. Now, God's names are *much* more descriptive and meaningful, but you get the idea. Each name above points to an aspect of who God is. But there is a name that is the greatest name of all for God, one that encompasses all of who he is at once.

Any time we see the word *Lord* in small caps in the Bible, it's an indicator that the translator intends for it to be a usage of God's sacred, very holy Name. This Name is often written as YHWH, based on how it was recorded in Hebrew. Today, we often pronounce it as *Yahweh* or *Jehovah* when reading the Bible out loud—but in reality, no one quite knows how to pronounce YHWH. In fact, the Jewish people stopped saying this name altogether because they were afraid of saying it incorrectly and accidentally taking it in vain. That's how powerful they saw it to be. Today, the important part to remember is that YHWH is a holy name, and we need to be careful only to use this name with the most reverence and care.

How do we know what this name means?

Again, we don't know exactly, but biblical scholars have tried to intuit the answer based on how God describes the name in Exodus. Tasked with requesting the release of the enslaved Israelites, Moses wanted to know what name he should use when he speaks of God to the Israelites.

And God answered Moses.

"God said to Moses, 'I AM WHO I AM. This is what you are to say to the Israelites: I AM has sent me to you.'"

It sounds sort of like a riddle at first.

Have you ever had to list definitions of vocabulary words in English class? Oftentimes, we'll lose points if we try to define a term by using the same term. We can't say the definition of *love* is "to be loving." We can't say the definition of *adventure* is "to have an adventure." We have to point to other descriptions and references in order to define these words and build the full picture of their meaning.

But God, who defines all things, doesn't use a name anyone else can use. Unlike with us, where our names are not always unique, can change, and add only a tiny piece to our identities, when God chooses to reveal his true name, it's the entirety of his identity and unchangeable. This name shows there is nothing outside of God, and there's nothing he looks to for a sense of identity. God *is* identity. All definition, all of creation, and all identifiers have meaning because of who he is and because of what he set into motion.

All the other descriptive names—the Shepherd, the Healer, the Lord who provides—still apply, of course. But they derive their meaning from somewhere, and the source of this meaning is God himself. There would be no sheep to protect and care for without him as Shepherd; no healing without him as the ultimate Physician; and no fulfilling or provision without God pouring these things into our lives.

So, when God says, "I AM WHO I AM," it means he is the fullness of all good things we can and cannot put human words to, and he always will be, for all of eternity.

He's like no other—not like us and certainly not like any of the gods the Egyptians worshiped. When God told Moses, "I AM WHO I AM," that was true for that moment in time, and it's still true today.

We can be glad today because God is who he is; tomorrow we can wake up with the same gladness, because he'll still be who he is then too. Each day, from now through forever, we can be glad because these words will always be true: God is who he is.

Live

How does it make you feel to know that God is who he is? Do you think this is confusing or do you find it comforting? Look at all the other names God uses in Scripture, and think about how each of them points back to that great name: I AM WHO I AM. How does each concept point to an aspect of his character? Which descriptive name for God do you find the most comforting?

Pray

Dear Lord, I'm so glad you are who you are and that all good things are a result of what you have done. Thank you for showing up, and for making yourself knowable to us here on earth. I want to know you more than I ever have before. When I study your Word, give me insight into your character and help me see your heart throughout my life.

Think

God's heart is unchanging and eternal because he is who he is, and we can't define him any other way!

God Is Love

Dear friends, let us love one another, for love comes from God. Everyone who loves has been born of God and knows God. Whoever does not love does not know God, because God is love. This is how God showed his love among us: He sent his one and only Son into the world that we might live through him. This is love: not that we loved God, but that he loved us and sent his Son as an atoning sacrifice for our sins.

1 JOHN 4:7–10

How many times do you think you've sung "Jesus Loves Me" over the course of your lifetime? If you grew up going to church, you probably learned the song around the same time you learned how to say *Mama* or *Dada*. If someone says, "Jesus loves me," I'll bet your mind fills the rest in with, "this I know." For a lot of us, the words of this song flow so automatically that we don't even stop to let the song settle in our spirits, and we don't pause on the depth of the words when they speak about Jesus' love for us.

Jesus loves you!

But why?

We don't have anything particularly compelling to offer the God of the universe. Even when we offer our very best, the most wonderful things about ourselves, we still can't add anything to the magnificence of God. He lacks nothing, so we can't fill a need for him. We're the most magnificent of all his creation, to be sure ("Very good!" as he said in Genesis), but still . . .

69

there's nothing we can do to make ourselves more attractive to God. So why does he, the God who sprinkled glittering stars across the inky expanse of the sky with only his words, love us so deeply?

Because he *is* love.

First John 4:7–8 says, "Dear friends, let us love one another, for love comes from God. Everyone who loves has been born of God and knows God. Whoever does not love does not know God, because God is love."

God is loving, yes. But love is also who he is. Love is God's character, and how he chooses to show us his heart is through love.

But love seems like such an enormous, broad concept. We love donuts and llamas and summer vacations, and we also love our friends and our family, and we're supposed to love our enemies. But there's no comparison between the way we love summer vacation and the way we love our best friend. The two are totally different experiences.

To understand what the Bible means when it tells us God is love, we have to look to the rest of Scripture to see what the big picture of his love actually is. You've probably seen and heard a lot of 1 Corinthians 13. It's the chapter of the Bible people sometimes call "the love chapter," and it's often read at weddings. "Love is patient," it says, "love is kind. It does not envy, it does not boast, it is not proud. It does not dishonor others, it is not self-seeking, it is not easily angered, it keeps no record of wrongs. Love does not delight in evil but rejoices with the truth. It always protects, always trusts, always hopes, always perseveres. Love never fails."

Each of these characteristics give us more insight into who God is. He doesn't just do these things; he is all these things.

Patience, kindness, trust, hope—every single one of the qualities listed in 1 Corinthians 13 is an aspect of the nature of God. He's the source and creator and the perfection of all these things in our lives and in the world.

Sometimes it's hard to see love in the world, though. We all go through rough times and situations where we don't feel loved by God. If love always protects, then why did God let that person hurt me? If love is kind, then why does it feel like God is withholding good things from me?

Though it isn't easy, we can trust God's character and have confidence that he's loving in every way, even when our circumstances feel topsy-turvy. This is called faith, and it's pleasing to God. Clinging to his promises and his character, even when our hearts are broken or when we have to fight to trust, is faith. It's taking God at his word. He's already demonstrated his heart through the ultimate sacrifice of his Son, Jesus Christ. Faith is what we have and how we live in response to our trust in who God says he is.

Knowing about God gives us nice things to say. We may sound good to church friends, and we may sound good to ourselves. But knowing *about* God and knowing God (or being in relationship with him) are different things. It's easier to give up on faith when we aren't in a true relationship with God. When this happens, it's because we're trusting in who we've told ourselves God should be instead of who he's told us he actually is.

But being in a real relationship with God gives us the opportunity to know him. He keeps revealing himself to us time after time as we grow closer to him, experience more of him, and learn who he is as we trust him. Then, when we go through darkness or find ourselves at rock bottom, we can look to who he actually is, see his love and strength, and trust him to carry out his promises, no matter what that follow-through may look like to us through our human perception.

God's the only one who has a perfect, eternal perspective. Though we may not see a way, we know the God who makes ways through seas and through deserts. He did this already by giving us Jesus, putting the entirety of his love for us on full display.

Live

Where do you see God's love most vibrantly in your life? Which things do you wrestle with sometimes? Do you think you know about God already, or are you in relationship with him so he can show you who he truly is?

Pray

Dear God, thank you for being an example of perfect love. With everything going on in the world and in my life, I sometimes have a hard time trusting your love for me. But I know my feelings don't need to take priority over what you've said. Your Word is truth. Today, I choose to trust in who you are over the way I feel. Help me to have faith when times are difficult. I love you, and I'm grateful for you and for the example you've given me.

Think

God is love and, because he is love and I'm in relationship with him, I can know what real love is.

God's Heart for Creativity

For we are God's handiwork, created in Christ Jesus to do good works, which God prepared in advance for us to do.

EPHESIANS 2:10

Have you been to an art gallery or an art show at school? Every single piece of art is different.

We don't simply slap something pretty on a photocopier and call it good. We use color and texture and light to express beauty and longing and love through the things we create.

Just like each one of our lives are different, each of the things we create are unique as well. No two people use paint in the same exact way to depict the same exact thing. Even if two people have similar ideas, the end results are always, at the very least, slightly different from each other.

We aren't this way on accident. We're creative because our Creator is creative. Ephesians 2:10 says we are God's handiwork! Just like we pour ourselves into expressing our hearts through the things we love to do, God poured a piece of himself into us.

Even a glance outside reveals his creativity. No sunrise or sunset looks the same as the ones that came before them. During the day, the skies change every minute with new and different clouds. At night, when the skies grow black, billions of stars pattern the darkness. And those are just the ones we can see!

If we look through superpowered telescopes, there are even more. More galaxies filled with stars. In fact, scientists now believe there may be more than two trillion galaxies out there.[1] It's impossible to imagine anyone coming up with two trillion anything, but God has done it over and over again, and each galaxy is entirely unique and different.

Isaiah 40:25–26 says, "'To whom will you compare me? Or who is my equal?' says the Holy One. Lift up your eyes and look to the heavens: Who created all these? He who brings out the starry host one by one and calls forth each of them by name. Because of his great power and mighty strength, not one of them is missing."

Not only did God create all these galaxies and the stars within them—the number of which we can't even begin to understand—he's named them. And he remembers their names.

Why does he do things like make galaxies we'll never discover and name stars we'll never see? We wouldn't have known the difference if we'd started out with a world of nothingness, a world without animals and skyscapes and more varieties of flowers than we could ever dream up. He could have made a world lacking beauty, diversity, or creativity. But that isn't the way of our Creator, and we see the results of that decision every single day.

God creates to remind us of the beauty of diversity. Nothing on earth or in heaven is without variety. Whether it's different kinds of planets or different kinds of puppies or different kinds of people, there's a wide variety in nearly everything we experience. It's all meant to be here, and all of it adds beauty, interest, and delight to our lives. None of that happens by accident—it's all by the design of our creative God and his desire to show his

---

1   "A Universe of 2 Trillion Galaxies," Lindsay Brooke, Royal Astronomical Society, published on *Phys.org.*, January 16, 2017. *https://phys.org/news/2017-01-universe-trillion-galaxies.html*, accessed October 22, 2018.

heart to us, the pinnacle of his creation. We can't see everything God does with our physical eyes all the time, so he uses much of his literal creation, things we can see, to remind us of who he is.

God creates to assure us of his control over our circumstances and his power to do more than we can imagine. Can we make the stars exist or can we make the ocean keep waving in perfect time? In the book of Job, after Job has spoken up about all he's experienced, laying his feelings bare before God and other men, God speaks up.

He responds to Job and says, "Have you entered the storehouses of the snow or seen the storehouses of the hail, which I reserve for times of trouble, for days of war and battle? What is the way to the place where the lightning is dispersed, or the place where the east winds are scattered over the earth? Who cuts a channel for the torrents of rain, and a path for the thunderstorm, to water a land where no one lives, an uninhabited desert, to satisfy a desolate wasteland and make it sprout with grass?" (All of this is in Job 38. Read the whole chapter for a list of some other ways God shows off his creativity and power.)

Before we ever existed, God created things beyond our imagination. Though we constantly discover new things about the world we live in and about our universe, we'll never understand the depths of it all. But God does! We get to create too, because the good things we do reflect good things of him.

God creates, then he expresses big ideas to us through what he's made. If God hadn't created sheep, it would mean nothing to us when he says we're the sheep of his pasture and he's our Good Shepherd. If he hadn't created the stars, it would have meant nothing to Abraham when God said his descendants would outnumber the stars. If God hadn't created trees, we wouldn't be able to understand what it means when the Bible says wise people are like trees rooted by streams of water.

What God has created, he uses to help us know him and experience his heart for us even more.

Live

Do you think of yourself as a creative person? Even if you're a lover of systems and strategy instead of paintbrushes and play, there's still a piece of your heart that reflects God's creativity. In what ways do you see God's creativity reflected in your life? What do you appreciate most about his creativity?

Pray

Dear Lord, I want to know you better. Help me recognize your heart in all the things you've made and put in my path. Thank you for making this life so vibrant and lovely. Thank you for giving me so many ways to encounter you every day.

Think

Our Creator's heart has led to my world being more beautiful and diverse, so I can experience life in all things beautiful and diverse.

God's Shepherd's Heart

The LORD is my shepherd, I lack nothing. He makes me lie down in green pastures, he leads me beside quiet waters, he refreshes my soul. He guides me along the right paths for his name's sake. Even though I walk through the darkest valley, I will fear no evil, for you are with me; your rod and your staff, they comfort me.

PSALM 23:1-4

Have you wondered why humanity is often compared to sheep in the Bible? God could have chosen to compare us to any animal in the world. He could have said we're all like bears—strong, tall, and oozing bravado. Or he could have compared us to tropical birds, the ones that look like moving artwork and sing beautiful songs. But, no. Sheep. God calls us sheep.

Sheep don't seem like bright animals. They wander. They don't smell all that great. They don't have any cool defense mechanisms. So why did God choose to say we're like sheep so often? Maybe a piece of it has to do with what we have in common with sheep. After all, we wander too. We're liable to get into trouble when we seek the next big thing to satisfy our appetites.

But God doesn't call us sheep to insult us. We're the pinnacle of his creation, made on purpose, with love and care. This isn't his commentary about how little we can comprehend or how unwise we are in comparison to him.

Matthew 9:36 says, "When [Jesus] saw the crowds, he had compassion on them, because they were harassed and helpless, like sheep without a shepherd." Jesus had been traveling through villages, telling people about the kingdom of God and healing people. He said these words when he saw the enormous groups of people with varying needs, all of whom needed something, all of whom desperately wanted his attention. He was probably already exhausted, having been traveling and teaching. By this time, Jesus was in high demand!

But instead of looking at the crowds around him and being angry at their neediness, *he had compassion on them*. When he saw the crowds, he recognized that they were like sheep without a shepherd, and it moved his heart to the point that he joined them in their suffering (which is what true compassion is). It didn't move him toward irritation or toward guilt; the people and the states of their hearts moved him to compassion.

Jesus saw these people as sheep, and in John 10:11 he says, "I am the good shepherd. The good shepherd lays down his life for the sheep." These aren't the words of someone who thinks sheep are stupid.

We aren't likened to sheep so often because God thinks little of us. Instead, we're called sheep because of our relationship with the Good Shepherd. And there's something really special about the relationship between sheep and their shepherd.

If your knowledge of shepherding culture goes beyond a couple viewings of the movie *Babe*, then you probably have more insight into the sheep and shepherd relationship. But for the rest of us, we can learn a lot from Psalm 23, because it tells us about what a shepherd does for his sheep and, in particular, what *our* Shepherd does for us.

A shepherd provides for his sheep. A good shepherd knows where to lead his sheep so they have plenty of food, plenty of rest, and plenty of refreshment. He takes his sheep to green pastures and quiet waters where they're able to eat and drink their fill. He leads his sheep to a place where they can safely rest.

The purpose of his provision isn't just to keep the sheep from being hungry—he feeds them so they'll also be able to follow him on the next leg of their journey. The sheep rest and are refreshed, then they continue on the path toward their destination, led by their shepherd.

A shepherd guides his sheep. The shepherd knows where he's going, and he takes his sheep where they need to go so they have what they need. The sheep have no sense of direction on their own; it's not a commentary on their intelligence, just a statement of how they were created. But why would they need to know the paths when they have a trustworthy guide? Their shepherd knows the way, and for the sheep, this is good enough.

The shepherd also doesn't drive his sheep along the paths. He doesn't beat them and force them where they need to go. He leads the way, and the sheep—who trust him and know his voice—go with him.

A shepherd protects his sheep. Even though the sheep journey with and are protected by their shepherd, he knows the pathway isn't without its fair share of danger. Just because the shepherd accompanies his sheep, that doesn't mean there won't be predators, briars, or storms along the journey. But the shepherd is prepared for these things, and he carries a staff to protect his flock both from themselves and from anything that wants to hurt them.

When the pathway grows dark, the sheep don't run from their shepherd because he's allowed them to enter a dark place. They press in closer to him so they can anticipate his next steps and so they can be comforted by his strength. They know that, though the darkness is unpleasant, the best place for them is with their shepherd.

And the shepherd doesn't abandon his sheep in the dark, either. When they encounter a twist in the trail or a tunnel along the way, the good shepherd goes into the darkness first. Having experienced the darkness himself many times before, he leads his sheep through with compassion and gentleness, because he understands.

And when one of his sheep get lost, he goes to find it, even when the search is dangerous, because he values each one in his flock.

We are Jesus' flock. He, like a literal shepherd with literal sheep, knows each of us. Our faces and our quirks and our dependence upon him are a source of delight. We, like sheep, need to be reminded to eat and rest and prepare for our journeys. We need a leader who guides us down the best path toward our destination. And we need a protector who has been where we are and knows how to fight our enemies.

We have all of these things in our Good Shepherd, Jesus.

Live

Have you put much thought into the Lord as your Shepherd? Are you comforted by this name or are you confused? Look up other Bible verses that refer to God's people as his sheep for even more examples of his heart for his people.

Pray

Jesus, thank you for being my Good Shepherd. I'm grateful for the ways you provide for me, the ways you guide me, and the ways you protect me even when I'm unaware. It makes my heart feel loved to know you care about me so much that you come after me when I wander. Thank you for pursuing me every time I get lost.

Think

God cares for me so much that he, like a shepherd, will take perfect care of me, and leave the rest of the flock to find me when I lose my way.

God's Heart of a Parent

"But while he was still a long way off, his father saw him and was filled with compassion for him; he ran to his son, threw his arms around him and kissed him.

"The son said to him, 'Father, I have sinned against heaven and against you. I am no longer worthy to be called your son.'

"But the father said to his servants, 'Quick! Bring the best robe and put it on him. Put a ring on his finger and sandals on his feet. Bring the fattened calf and kill it. Let's have a feast and celebrate. For this son of mine was dead and is alive again; he was lost and is found.' So they began to celebrate."

LUKE 15:20–24

When the topic of parents comes up, you likely have strong feelings regarding yours. If they're the "Muffins with Mom" and "Donuts with Dad" type, showing up every time you need them and even sometimes you don't, you might have joy-filled, warm feelings.

Or your relationship with your parents might be less . . . spectacular. Since pain is a very real part of life, your parents may have experienced pain they didn't know how to handle, and it may deeply influence how they treat you.

It's also possible that you have the kind of relationship with your parents that lands somewhere in the middle of the two—sort of complicated at times, but still an all-around decent relationship.

Whatever we think and feel about our relationships with

our parents, it can drastically affect how we think and feel about God. It's easier for us to trust God's love and care for us if we've had trustworthy relationships with our parents even early on in childhood. But if we've been hurt by or lacked protection from our parents throughout our lives, we may superimpose those attributes over the true nature of God's heart.

God's heart is that of a perfect parent. And, in addition to having the heart of a perfect parent, he also fills in everything we lack in our relationships with our biological or adoptive parents. He shows us throughout Scripture—verse after verse, story after story—how he loves us in the same way a good parent loves her child.

God's parent-heart is protective of us. Psalm 91:4 says God covers us with his feathers and gives us refuge under his wings. He watches over us like a mother bird watches over her chicks, providing shelter and his presence even in times of trouble.

Being kept close and warm is wonderful, but sometimes protection doesn't feel great. Have you ever seen a toddler throwing a tantrum in the parking lot after running away, while Mom or Dad drag them back toward safety? When we experience discipline, from our parents or from God, it's not pleasant. But discipline is a form of protection given to us by God, who loves us and wants only the best for us. He doesn't use discipline as a tool to bring shame or manipulate us; only to protect us and to help us grow into greater strength and character.

God's parent-heart is patient toward us. In the story of the prodigal son, a parable Jesus told to illustrate God's love for his children, we clearly see how God remains patient toward us even when we take matters into our own hands, living in ways that highlight our selfishness and our tendencies toward entitlement.

The story is about two sons and their relationships with their father. No matter what the younger son did—and he did a lot of dumb stuff—his father waited for him to come home. When the younger son finally came home, the father celebrated his return. But the older brother was ticked about the celebration. He didn't like the fact that they threw a party for someone whose behavior had been so careless and unloving, when he'd been steady and diligent the whole time.

But in spite of the older son's reaction to his brother's return, their father still held space for his more obedient son at the celebration and longed for him to be there.

No matter what we do or how we act, God is patient toward us and he will *always* celebrate our return, many times over if needed.

God's parent-heart provides for us. There's no greater example of God's provision for us than his provision of Jesus Christ. We've been given the sacrifice necessary to satisfy God's heart of justice, through absolutely nothing we could do on our own.

God continues to provide for us in other ways because he is good and because he cares for us like good parents care for their children. Second Peter 1:3 says, "[God's] divine power has given us everything we need for a godly life through our knowledge of him who called us by his own glory and goodness." We might wonder if God's always providing because we don't always see the bigger picture, but we can trust him and take him at his word. He is Jehovah-Jireh, and he provides!

God's parent-heart is proud of us. If God had a refrigerator, your picture would be plastered all over it. He takes such great delight in you, and he wouldn't have made you otherwise! You're his child, and he cherishes you exactly as you are. When he sees you enjoy the gifts he wove into the fabric of your being, it brings him delight. He's drawn to you with the purest love. His heart is for you, and his thoughts are about you. Psalm 139:17–18 says, "How precious to me are your thoughts, God! How vast is the sum of them! Were I to count them, they would outnumber the grains of sand."

You are his creation, and he's so pleased with you!

Live

In what ways do you think your relationship with your parents has affected your relationship with God? Do you feel like there are more positive or negative influences shaping how you see God in your life? How do you think God is different from your parents, and how do you think they're like him?

Pray

Father God, your protection, your patience, and your provision are all gifts. Step into my story and smooth over the places where I feel injured by my relationship with my parents—things that may be keeping my heart from fully trusting in you. Help me to fully experience you where I feel my relationships are lacking.

Think

God's heart toward me is like that of a perfect parent's heart; he protects, he is patient, he provides, and he is pleased with me.

God's Heart for Peace

Do not be anxious about anything, but in every situation, by prayer and petition, with thanksgiving, present your requests to God. And the peace of God, which transcends all understanding, will guard your hearts and your minds in Christ Jesus.

PHILIPPIANS 4:6–7

Maybe you've seen these words on a bumper sticker or on a T-shirt: "Know Jesus, Know Peace." It's a pithy way to express a deep truth, for sure. But it's easy to remember, and we understand what it means. Or do we?

What comes to mind when you think of peace?

Some of us may immediately imagine a vacation, one on a tropical island where we get to sit in a hammock next to a large stack of books and a tall glass of iced tea. No school or work or any of the obligations we're responsible for! It does sound very peaceful.

Or we might go in a less literal direction, and our hearts long for the absence of a tough situation we're going through. All we can think about is the fact our lives would be so much easier without the turmoil of whatever it is that's wreaking havoc on our days. Whether we battle anxiety or watch a loved one struggle with an addiction, when we think of peace, we may long for a time when those things simply don't exist anymore.

Jesus said to the disciples, "Peace I leave with you; my peace I give you. I do not give to you as the world gives. Do not let your hearts be troubled and do not be afraid" (John 14:27). I wonder if, at those moments, the disciples' minds skipped to relaxing vacations and leaving behind their hardest circumstances too. Maybe they felt the burdens in their hearts lift just a little as they imagined what it would feel like if all their troubles somehow melted away. Jesus himself, after all, told them he would give them peace, so it would seem they'd be hopeful for easier days ahead.

But then Jesus was crucified, and any peace they'd felt before probably felt farther away than ever before. Even after Jesus was resurrected and went back to heaven, things were still difficult for the disciples. A few of them were also crucified. Others were exiled. Some were stoned. None of these things are remotely peaceful. We have to wonder if even the disciples started to doubt if the peace Jesus offered really had truth to it.

When we come up against hard times, what is peace anyway if we wake up the next morning to just as much chaos as we experienced when we went to bed the night before?

A day is coming when our struggles will no longer cause us pain. Revelation 21:4 says, "'He will wipe every tear from their eyes. There will be no more death' or mourning or crying or pain, for the old order of things has passed away." But that's in heaven, when we're reunited with our Father and get to spend the rest of eternity experiencing the ultimate, forever peace with him.

So, what do we do in the "right now"? Is peace possible for us here on earth?

Yes, of course! Jesus also told the disciples, "In this world you will have trouble." That part makes sense. We know trouble. All it takes is a glance at a newsfeed or the comments section of any post on a news website for us to see trouble overflowing. But Jesus doesn't stop there, at the hardship. After he reminded the disciples there would be adversity, he said something wonderful: "But take heart! I have overcome the world" (John 16:33).

Peace isn't the absence of chaos in our circumstances, but the absence of chaos in our hearts because we are well acquainted with the One who has overcome the world and we trust him. Though we go through some seriously scary times, we can count on the fact we know what's true.

> We know God is for us (Romans 8:31).
> We know his Word will stand forever (Matthew 24:35).
> We know he cares for us (Luke 12:22–31).
> We know we have not been abandoned (Deuteronomy 31:6).
> We know we have great hope because Jesus has gone before us (Hebrews 6:18–20).

Lavished all over Scripture are these promises, and many more, about who God is and what he's done. We can trust what God's said to us through the pages of his Word, even if our circumstances try to tell us otherwise.

Having peace doesn't mean we get really good at pretending our tough things don't exist or that we don't have bad feelings about the chaos we experience. Peace is trusting that God knows the ins and outs of our lives and that he will somehow, some way, use everything to bring about good for his kingdom.

One of God's names is Jehovah Shalom, or "The Lord is Peace." Even if we don't know any of the answers to our life's hardest questions or have the fixes to our most difficult problems, we know Jesus. When our hearts feel like they're in turmoil, we keep inviting him in there to deal with the things we can't.

Philippians 4:6–7 says, "Do not be anxious about anything, but in every situation, by prayer and petition, with thanksgiving, present your requests to God. And the peace of God, which transcends all understanding, will guard your hearts and your minds in Christ Jesus." There's no need to judge ourselves for feeling anxious or overwhelmed—those feelings are simply a reminder to call on Jesus. It's entirely because of him that we can have peace at all.

So when we feel overwhelmed with uncertainty or difficulty or chaos, peace means we don't have to flail and fight to claw our way out of it. This world has trouble, after all. But that's not the end of the story.

We know Jehovah Shalom, the Lord is Peace. And even when we can't see a way out of the chaos in our lives and even if we don't know how to fix it, we know Jesus.

Live

What circumstances cause you to feel caught up in turmoil today? Where do you feel Jesus is right now in your life? There is no wrong answer to this question. While the truth is Jesus is by your side in the midst of your chaos, your feelings may be telling you otherwise. That's okay! It's an opportunity to remind your heart of the truth even when the feelings aren't there yet.

Pray

Dear Jesus, I'm glad you understand the trouble of this world. You know I've gone through some messed-up stuff. Sometimes I'm not sure how to handle everything. But today, I want to choose to put my trust in your heart of peace. It's because of you that I can have peace at all. Please still the chaos in my heart. Help me trust that you are who you say you are even when life is messy.

Think

God's heart is my perfect source of peace because I can trust him to hold me up even in the middle of my toughest circumstances.

God's Advocate Heart

[Jesus said,] "If you love me, keep my commands.
And I will ask the Father, and he will give you
another advocate to help you and be with you
forever—the Spirit of truth. The world cannot accept
him, because it neither sees him nor knows him.
But you know him, for he lives with you and will be
in you. I will not leave you as orphans; I will come to
you. Before long, the world will not see me anymore,
but you will see me. Because I live, you also will live.
On that day you will realize that I am in my Father,
and you are in me, and I am in you. Whoever has my
commands and keeps them is the one who loves me.
The one who loves me will be loved by my Father,
and I too will love them and show myself to them."

JOHN 14:15-21

When Jesus spoke to his disciples about the Holy Spirit, you have to wonder what they thought he was referring to, since they'd never experienced the Holy Spirit before. Jesus told them about the Holy Spirit while they were together at the Last Supper. A confusing time for the disciples, for sure! They'd experienced real life with him, sharing food, walking miles and miles of hot, dusty dirt roads together—and then all of a sudden, he told them he was leaving them, but they shouldn't worry because the Spirit of truth would be with them instead.

It must have been a record-scratch sort of moment, causing their hearts and thoughts to stumble over what Jesus told them.

An advocate? The Spirit of truth? What did that even mean?

Today, we have a better idea of who Jesus was talking about because we experience the Holy Spirit's work in our hearts as we get to know God. We still have a hard time understanding everything Jesus was trying to tell us, though, because as knowable as God is to us, there will always be things about him that just don't make sense from our perspectives.

The word *advocate* is one of the terms that can be hard to understand. But biblical scholars have also translated the word as *counselor*—a word that may be a little easier to comprehend, since there are many types of counselors in our world. Maybe if we look at those people who are advocates/counselors in our lives, we'll be able to piece together an idea as to how the Holy Spirit continues to be a counselor to us.

Legal Counselors

When we struggle to understand the law, there's no one better to help us comprehend all the nuances than a legal counselor who's studied hard and knows where the boundaries lie. (Legal counselors are also called attorneys or lawyers, and there are many good ones in the world!) These are the people who guide us as we follow the law, who point out where we may be in violation of the law, who give us advice on how to align ourselves with the law, and who push for justice in the world.

The Holy Spirit sometimes serves as a counselor for us in this way too. Have you ever felt convicted in your heart when you've sinned against God? That's the Holy Spirit reminding us where God's good boundaries lie and urging us toward repentance (or turning away from) our sin. We're able to follow God's commands and to obey him because of the Holy Spirit's presence in our lives.

High School Counselors

High school counselors offer direction and advice to us when we need to make important decisions about our future. They know about lots of different paths we can pursue, and they can point out the pros and cons of each, especially as they relate to our specific situations in life.

We have a great, omniscient (all-knowing) guide in the Holy Spirit. Proverbs 16:9 says, "In their hearts humans plan their course, but the LORD establishes their steps." He knows all the paths we could take, and he establishes our steps, guiding us as we seek his advice and wisdom. When we ask God for wisdom and understanding to make important decisions, he directs our path through the leading of the Holy Spirit, who works as a counselor in our hearts, giving us advice as we go through life.

Camp Counselors

Camp counselors are often fun-loving, adventurous, and passionate about life. They aren't afraid to get messy and go all in. A good camp counselor spends lots of time with her campers and watches out for them, guiding them away from potential danger and helping them have fun in the process.

Our God is also fun-loving, adventurous, and passionate about life! Who else would have instilled in us a desire to chase after big dreams besides a God who loves the journey and adventure of it all? Our lives were not meant to be flat, boring, one-note experiences. Instead, we have a fun-loving, adventurous, passionate-about-life Holy Spirit who leads us on a journey of discovery and joy, while also protecting us from experiences that could harm us in the end.

Therapeutic Counselors

For some people, going to counseling feels shameful. When that is the case, it's often because we think we should be able to pull our lives together without the help of anyone else. But God has given certain individuals wisdom, empathy, and excellent listening skills so they can be a blessing and a help in our lives.

Quality therapeutic counselors spend time with us and listen to our stories—all the good parts and all the really difficult parts. They are trustworthy, guarding the things we've shared. Therapeutic counselors sit with us as we experience all ranges of emotions, from joy to grief to anger to jealousy. After listening and making sure we feel heard, they help us sort through our blind spots and encourage us to discover healthier ways to relate to ourselves and to others.

There's no greater therapeutic counselor than the Holy Spirit. He's with us at all times, in all circumstances, and he understands our feelings even better than we do. Our hearts are safe with the Holy Spirit because he is more trustworthy than anyone else could ever be. And he's gracious to gently lead us toward healing and wholeness in every area of our lives.

God's Spirit is timeless and true, active in our lives and in our hearts. When we step into faith, we start out on a journey with him, and we can trust that he will counsel and comfort us through every experience we have.

Live

How do you see the Holy Spirit as an active participant in your life? Do you feel like you've experienced a certain aspect of his counsel more than the others? How would you like to partner more with the Holy Spirit right now?

Pray

Holy Spirit, I pray that you would make me more aware of all the ways you're active in my life today. I want to notice the ways you speak into my heart. Help me recognize your voice, whether you're asking me to do something new or you're wanting to show off how much you love me.

Think

God wishes to speak into my life as often as I will listen.

God's Heart for the Journey

Trust in the LORD with all your heart and lean not on
your own understanding; in all your ways submit to
him, and he will make your paths straight.

PROVERBS 3:5–6

Everything that has life is meant to grow. After babies are born, we take them back to the doctor periodically so they can be weighed and examined to make sure they're continuing to develop. If a child doesn't grow and develop in a healthy way, they're diagnosed with a condition called "failure to thrive."

Just like our bodies, our hearts can experience a "failure to thrive." Our bodies and our spirits—or our hearts—were both created with growth in mind. While our bodies need food in order to develop and mature, our hearts require a journey.

God designed us this way. He created us to start as babies and, over time, slowly become our adult selves, hitting milestones along the way. If this is the way he made our bodies to be from the beginning, it makes sense that he would also set our hearts on a similar journey of growth and thriving.

While we're alive, our purpose is to keep journeying with God. No matter where the twists and turns of our lives take us, we trust the Lord, who is our guide throughout the entire experience. The trusting and the journeying together with God helps us become the women he intends for us to be, women after his own heart.

When we go on a new journey of any kind, we make lots of new discoveries when we're active participants in the expedition.

All journeys, good and difficult, take us away from the routine experiences of our everyday lives and prime our hearts to learn new things. A new journey shakes us up and reminds us that our lives aren't always predictable or comfortable.

Have you ever been camping in the wilderness? Tent life isn't usually very glamorous. Sleeping on the ground is uncomfortable, and none of us feel particularly fresh and lovely after a few days without running water. But the discomfort and stripping away of all our usual amenities has a way of reminding us of what really matters and where our focus needs to stay.

Our lives may feel long and mundane, but James 4:14 says we're a mist that appears for a little while before vanishing. Every day is an opportunity to commit to the journey and remember what really matters.

While we move forward on our journeys, we also have to focus on our Guide, the Lord. Any other guide will lead us over cliffs or into danger without a reason. But Proverbs 3:5–6 says we have a better guide, one who's trustworthy and who knows where we're going. "Trust in the Lord," it says, "with all your heart and lean not on your own understanding; in all your ways submit to him, and he will make your paths straight."

Though we may feel like experts on our own lives, most of us would probably agree that we still have no idea where we're going. We can set goals and plan ahead, but God's the only one who knows how things are going to work out for us ten years from now or even tomorrow. It doesn't matter how much we try to prepare ourselves; we can only plan for so much.

But when we trust God as our Guide, we gain his perspective and the benefit of his wisdom. While we can't predict where our journeys will take us, God knows exactly where we need to head. He's well acquainted with the terrain even when we're clueless. In fact, he's placed us where we are "for such a time as this," to accomplish the purpose he set out.

God, like a good trail guide, knows what to look out for. He's aware of the road ahead, and he's prepared for the challenges and triumphs coming our way. Because of this, he prepares us as well.

When we equip ourselves for a physical journey, it usually involves some sort of training. People who hike the entire Appalachian Trail don't show up at the trailhead in their new hiking boots and move through the whole trail in a couple of weeks. They have to train ahead of time to make sure their bodies and spirits can handle the trek, and they have to break in their boots and their packs. That preparation takes a lot of hard work and a lot of dedication over the course of many months. Without this discipline, they'd have to quit before reaching the end of the trail or they might find themselves in severe danger.

Training is often unpleasant. Sometimes the perseverance and patience God requires of us is a tool he's using to prepare us for what's ahead in our journeys. It's hard work to remain faithful and to keep trusting God our Guide in the middle of our particularly tough times, but we don't know what we'll encounter in the future. What may be tough now might have been impossible were it not for the "training" we've already undergone alongside our good Guide.

We all change as we journey. Every step along the way is an opportunity for growth and strength building, but we have to start somewhere. When we're in the middle of the journey, it does us no good to look back on ourselves as we were when we just began and feel shame and disgust for that past self. God delights in our beginnings in the same way that he delights in our middles and in our endings. As long as we keep our eyes and our hearts on him, we'll stay where we need to be. Our Good Guide beckons us onward, right beside us the entire time.

Just because we know God and trust him to make our paths straight, that doesn't mean our paths will be easy. Some straight paths go straight up, and anybody who's climbed straight up the side of a fourteener—a mountain that's fourteen thousand feet or more in elevation—will tell you that your lungs and legs burn more going straight up than if you were winding around.

When God has made our paths straight, we're able to see our destination, which is residing with him in his presence. We know where we're going to end up and, because we know where we're going, we can keep going even though the journey is sometimes challenging.

Live

At this moment in your life's journey, do you feel confident in the Lord as your Good Guide? Are you having trouble trusting him to be with you on your journey? Or are you enjoying where you are right now?

Pray

Dear God, I'm glad you know my entire journey from beginning to end, including all the details and how I need to train for what's ahead. Would you give me the strength and the fortitude I need to journey well? You are my trustworthy Guide, and I want to enjoy this journey with you leading me every step of the way. Please correct me when I start to step off the path into danger. Show me all the beauty surrounding me with every step we take together.

Think

God's desire is to be my Good Guide, and he knows the beginning, middle, and end of my earthly journey. I can be confident in his ability to lead me where I need to go.

God's Trustworthy Heart

The LORD is a refuge for the oppressed, a stronghold
in times of trouble. Those who know your name trust
in you, for you, LORD, have never forsaken those who
seek you.

PSALM 9:9–10

Before lifeguards can swing their whistles at our neighborhood pools, they have to go through extensive lifeguard
training. They learn how to carry out water rescues, how
to administer CPR and first aid, and how to care for spinal and
head injuries. By the end of their training, lifeguards should be
well equipped to help in the event of an emergency at the pool,
beach, or water park where they work.

Why don't the lifeguards just hop into the pool and swim
beside us to do their jobs? It seems like if they did, they might
be able to help more quickly if an emergency happened because
they'd already be right there. Instead, they climb up on lifeguard
stands and take a seat there, or they stand on the edge of the
pool, where they watch in shifts.

But lifeguards sitting high above the pool in their chairs or
standing on the edge have a much better vantage point than anybody already in the water. They see things the rest of us aren't
able to see while we're splashing around. If there's danger below,
like a shallow pool bottom or a weak swimmer, they're able to
spot it quickly before jumping in to help if needed.

We trust the lifeguards to see what we can't. Their perspective makes all the difference.

God also has a different perspective than we do. One of the

words we use to describe him is *omnipresent*. This means he's able to be everywhere at once, even across time. His perspective allows him to see the fullness of everything, from beginning to end, in our lives and in the lives of everyone else who has ever existed. Because of who he is and because of the power he has, we trust God to see what we can't.

Trust isn't an easy, follow-the-right-steps-and-we-have-it-all-down sort of thing, though. Think about your relationships now. People who should have been there for us betray us. A loved one who was supposed to care and be supportive doesn't and isn't. Trustworthy relationships aren't always a part of our stories, and sometimes we walk around wounded and distrusting because of how these relationships have impacted our lives. We let this seep into our relationships with God too, because it's what we know.

But God is literally the only one who deserves our whole-hearted trust. When we trust him, we start to see things from a more eternal perspective like he does. When we trust God's heart and his care for us, we relate better, we serve better, and we love better.

And Satan knows this. That's why he works so hard to erode our ability to trust God's heart for us. If he can erode our trust in God's heart, then everything else gets obscured.

If we can't trust that God is always working for our good, then we'll continually question his character when we experience hard times. If we can't trust God's heart wants to bring us into relationship with him, then Jesus' sacrifice is just a story. If we can't trust that God is for our freedom, then we might see temptations as things a boring, out-of-touch dictator just wants to keep from us.

To trust God more, we have to get to know him better,

spending time with him and learning his heart, so when we hear lies, we catch them immediately instead of thinking on them and wondering if maybe they're more accurate than what God says to us. This is how Satan worked his way into Eve's world at the very beginning of the earth. He attacked God's character when he said, "Did God really say . . ." And suddenly Eve began to distrust God's heart and the guidance he gave for her life. Satan has obscured the truth from people ever since.

Sometimes he even does this by telling us lies about trust itself. Some of us are convinced that in order to trust God, we have to understand everything about him. We think we have to figure out the really confusing parts of Scripture, and we have to understand why bad things happen in the world, and why bad things have happened to us. But trust is not equal to understanding.

If the lifeguard jumps into the deep end of the pool, and we're in the shallow end, we may not understand why they're leaping but we can still trust they have a good reason to do so. Trusting means we have assurance that the person in whom we're putting our faith has a greater understanding of what's going on than we do.

Trust also doesn't mean we have happy feelings all the time. Sometimes trusting God feels gritty and messy and it plain doesn't make sense. But we do it anyway because we know what the Bible says about him and who he is.

We can speak freely with God and pour out our hearts to him. Our feelings don't scare God, and he's not going to be shocked when we lay it all out there. Feelings are valuable because they tell us something in our spirit needs attention, but they aren't always accurate depictions of reality. We honor God when we choose not to let our feelings be our truth.

When we choose to believe God is greater than our questions or greater than our experiences, it sends our hearts an important message: he is trustworthy, and we can trust him!

Live

Is there something keeping you from fully trusting God? Is that thing true or trustworthy? How have your relationships made it easier or more difficult for you to trust God?

Pray

Lord, trusting you isn't easy. I don't understand a lot of things, and I don't like when things don't make sense. Today, I'm choosing to trust that you are who you say you are even if my feelings haven't caught up yet. Remind me of your faithfulness. Bring to mind all the ways you've proven your trustworthiness to me in the past, and help me to recognize your faithfulness in real time as I experience it. Call out the lies I'm believing, and replace those lies with truth.

Think

God's heart is trustworthy, and I can trust him in all circumstances, even the ones that seem truly rotten.

God's Faithful Heart

Because of the LORD's great love we are not consumed, for his compassions never fail. They are new every morning; great is your faithfulness.

LAMENTATIONS 3:22–23

Stories stick with us. We can study for history tests by writing down dates and memorizing timelines and names, but we'll probably forget about all those things a couple of weeks after the test is over. But if we pay attention to the story of how things happened, who was involved, and when and where the events played out, we'll remember the narrative for much longer. When story is involved, the message we learn from it is retained much deeper in our hearts and minds.

Think about the stories we tell little kids even when they're still too young to speak. We read them "Beauty and the Beast," and they learn the heart is the true essence of a person, more so than their appearance. They huff and puff and blow houses down along with the Big Bad Wolf and learn that diligence and hard work are more beneficial than laziness. If anyone read you "The Three Little Pigs" when you were a kid, it's not likely that you've forgotten the story. Story digs in and doesn't let go.

Maybe this is why God uses story so often in the Bible. When Jesus had a point to make, he'd often use a parable, a story that illustrates a moral or lesson in a relatable way. It's how he communicated to everyone who wanted to listen to the truth about God's desire to come for us.

Luke 15 is a whole chapter of parables—the Parable of the Lost Sheep, the Parable of the Lost Coin, and the Parable of the

Lost Son (who you may know as the prodigal son). God does tell us he will never stop loving us (Romans 8:35–39 makes it clear), but he also *shows* us what that looks like.

When we imagine a shepherd running to find the single lost sheep, even though he has ninety-nine others, we can almost feel his overwhelming love for and dedication to that single sheep. And when we think about the woman tearing apart her home to find her lost coin, the thing she values the most, it adds extra weight to the knowledge that God values us even more. And with the parable of the prodigal son—it's a picture of God's enduring love for his kids, even those of us whose actions aren't so loving.

Sometimes God bypasses the parables and jumps into real life, using narratives about heroes of our faith, such as Abraham and Rahab and David. Every single story in the Bible, whether it's a parable or real life, teaches us something important about God and his heart for us.

The story of Hosea is one of those important stories, and it's recorded in a book named after the man himself. God asked Hosea to get married. Hosea must have been a man who followed the Lord closely because God knew Hosea would be obedient to the odd request. It wouldn't have been much of a strange command if God had asked Hosea to find a godly woman to be his wife. Instead, God asked Hosea to find a prostitute. And so Hosea found Gomer, a woman with whom he fell deeply in love, a woman who didn't care about him enough to be a faithful wife.

It seems bizarre, doesn't it, that God would ask this of Hosea? It must have been incredibly painful for Hosea to watch his wife turn to other men and abandon him and their children. In spite of what Gomer does, the ways she wounds Hosea and their children, and how she ignores the love lavished upon her,

God tells Hosea to keep going to her. Keep pursuing Gomer. Run after her, find her, seek her out, don't leave her. No matter what happened, Hosea was to love Gomer and be faithful to her.

Doesn't that seem unfair? Didn't Hosea's heart matter? Of course it mattered! But God trusted Hosea to live out a story bigger than himself, one that would show Gomer, the Israelites, and us a true picture of God's heart for us.

God told Hosea, "Go, show your love to your wife again, though she is loved by another man and is an adulteress. Love her as the LORD loves the Israelites . . ."

And there's the point of the whole story, isn't it? Love her as the Lord loves his people. This isn't a story about one man's broken heart. It was a story meant to show the Israelites how much God loved them, even though they kept going after idols and sinning instead of staying true to God and recognizing his love. And today it remains a story about how we act around God and how he keeps pursuing us, how he seeks us out, how he doesn't leave us. No matter how we behave or choose to turn away from his love, God's love for us endures. He keeps coming back for us. And Jesus is the result of God's enduring pursuit of our hearts.

Lamentations 3:22–23 says, "Because of the LORD's great love we are not consumed, for his compassions never fail. They are new every morning; great is your faithfulness."

Every morning the sun rises, whether we see it or not. Over the whole history of our planet, the sun has never not risen. There's a steady rhythm to its presence in our lives. Nothing we do will ever change the fact that the sun rises and the sun sets. God's love for us is even more consistent than the sunrise and sunset. After the world is gone, his love for us will still remain.

The story God has written since the beginning of time, the same one he continues to write today, will always point us back to the faithful love he has for us. There's nothing we can do to cause him to end his relentless pursuit of our hearts.

Live

How does it feel to know that God is pursuing you every day? Do you truly believe he's willing to endure everything to pursue your heart? What other stories in the Bible can you think of that remind you of God's faithful heart?

Pray

Dear Lord, I don't understand how you can love me all the time, but I'm grateful for it. Thank you for pursuing me even when I'm not all that lovely. Today, help me to be even more aware of all the ways you're in pursuit of my heart. Help me to recognize the ways you reach out and call me toward your love every day.

Think

There's nothing more steady or dependable than God's faithful love for me and his constant pursuit of my heart.

God's Heart for Connection

Therefore, since we have a great high priest who
has ascended into heaven, Jesus the Son of God,
let us hold firmly to the faith we profess. For we do
not have a high priest who is unable to empathize
with our weaknesses, but we have one who has been
tempted in every way, just as we are—yet he did not
sin. Let us then approach God's throne of grace with
confidence, so that we may receive mercy and find
grace to help us in our time of need.

HEBREWS 4:14–16

Have you ever poured your heart out to a friend or family member, laying all the gory details out there, baring your soul, only to ask a question and realize that person . . . isn't really listening at all? Or worse, maybe they were listening, but all they have to say in response is that your experience "wasn't that big of a deal" or it is something you should "get over." Even when we have exciting news to share, this sometimes happens.

People who have a hard time sympathizing miss out on making a heart connection during a time when connection is really essential.

No matter the reason behind the lack of connection, it hurts when we run into this lack of emotional support. We feel unheard, unseen, and totally misunderstood. It's incredibly painful when someone we've trusted with our hearts seems unable to "go there" with us, whether we're happy or hurting.

It sounds almost trite to say Jesus will always "go there"

with us, but it's the truth. We may know in our minds that God understands what we're going through, but sometimes that seems like the Sunday school answer instead of the reality of our lives.

But this is one of the great truths of our faith. God, instead of turning away and disconnecting his heart from ours, chose to join us in our experiences through Jesus, who empathizes with us in all that we go through. Empathizing is another layer of knowing beyond sympathizing, because the one who can empathize is the one who knows our experience, because they've been through the same things. They love us and can connect with us from a place of knowing. And this is what Jesus does.

Reread the verse that started this chapter, Hebrews 4:14–16. Jesus is the high priest these verses refer to. A high priest is one who goes before God on our behalf. Prior to Jesus, men needed to serve in that place, as the ones to offer sacrifice and go to God on behalf of those seeking the Lord. But now, thanks to his ultimate sacrifice on the cross, Jesus is our high priest, the ultimate heart connection between us and God. And even though he's entirely set apart from us because he didn't sin, he still completely understands every temptation we've ever had. He understands our feelings, our hurts, our happiness, and our deepest longings. There's nothing in our lives Jesus cannot understand.

Sometimes we can feel like God's unreachable to us, that he set the world into motion and left us here to work out the rest of our lives alone. He could have chosen to do that, for sure.

God could have legitimately decided he wanted absolutely nothing to do with us, especially after sin came into the world, but he didn't. Instead, he always has and always will do everything he can to draw us back into relationship with himself.

God's so concerned with being reachable and available to us that he sent us Jesus. Because of Jesus, there's no distance anymore.

As our great high priest, the perfect one who goes before God on our behalf, Jesus is wholly equipped to understand even the most confusing thoughts and feelings our hearts experience throughout our lives. Other people may distance themselves from us when our situations feel messy or baffling, but Jesus isn't afraid of these times.

Remember how Jesus interacted with people during his time on earth? He had in-depth conversations with people whose most "authentic" connections had been entirely counterfeit, leading them away from peace and nearness with God. Until they met Jesus!

For example, the woman at the well wanted to be understood in her relationships, perhaps hoping that at least one of her husbands would risk connecting with her heart enough to fulfill the emptiness she'd had her entire life. When she met Jesus, he saw through the counterfeit connections she'd been relying on and went straight to the heart of the matter—an offer of himself, the Living Water. And it changed her life.

Our high priest, Jesus, allows us to confess everything to him, from our most petty thoughts to our darkest, most hurtful actions. There's no need to hold anything back because he's well equipped to hear our confessions and give us grace and forgiveness where we once carried sin. We have the freedom to share it all with him. And with Jesus in this place, we can have open, candid conversation.

Where we experience disappointment, pain, and failure, Jesus gives us another opportunity for connection with our Father's heart. He isn't repelled by our pain, even the pain we've brought upon ourselves, and is instead able to bear the weight of it himself. He's able to sit with us when we need someone who understands.

While God is often a mystery to us, so marvelous and so much more than we can fathom, we are no mystery to him. As the creator of our abilities to feel and process and love and live, he completely understands every piece of our hearts and longs to connect with us there. Who better to understand us than the one who dreamed us up in the first place?

Live

Do you believe God empathizes with what you're going through, or do you feel like he has forgotten about you? What are some areas of your life where you don't feel very understood? How can you see God meeting you in those places and connecting with you?

Pray

Dear Jesus, thank you for being the perfect high priest who goes to God our Father on my behalf. I know without you I would have no hope for true connection. Open my eyes to the ways I may be clinging to counterfeit connections, and show me how I can better rely on you to fulfill the longings I have in my heart.

Think

God longs to connect with me on a heart level, and one way he does that is through empathizing with everything I go through.

God's Heart for Prayer

I call on you, my God, for you will answer me; turn your ear to me and hear my prayer. Show me the wonders of your great love, you who save by your right hand those who take refuge in you from their foes. Keep me as the apple of your eye; hide me in the shadow of your wings.

PSALM 17:6–8

You probably know your best friend really well, better than most people do. Lots of people may be aware of her eye color or where she was born, but you could list off so much more. In your mental friendship filing cabinet, you store information about what air freshener she uses in her car, which words make her cringe, and the exact combination of food and movies to pull her out of the doldrums after a breakup. These aren't things a casual acquaintance would know.

Getting to know someone doesn't happen in a vacuum, though. Before you hit best friend level, there are usually lots of conversations and shared experiences. Through these conversations and experiences, you become closer to each other.

Our relationship with God deepens and grows stronger when we spend time with him the way we would spend time with a friend, having conversations and recognizing the ways he's present in our life.

He already sees us, knows us, and calls us the best of his creation. He deeply desires for us to know him too and to experience a deep and wonderful friendship with him.

God enjoys the time we spend with him similar to the way

we enjoy time hanging out with the people we love. And while we're praying (having a conversation), we learn new things about God. The act of prayer is a gift God's given to us to help us connect with him.

Prayer Is a Way for Us to Share Our Concerns with Our Father Who Cares

We may feel silly praying about "little" things, even if they're important to us. When we're aware of all the difficult things in the world, sometimes it seems like we have no right to pray about the things that trouble our hearts. Maybe you've even said, "It's not a big deal compared to . . ." and decided not to pray about something, even though you're sad or hurt by it.

But God's power and resources are infinite. With a glance, he can split an ocean in half or heal a sick pet. Both are equally possible for him if he chooses to do so. Because prayer is all about us connecting with our Creator, he's not upset when we pour our hearts out to him, even if the things we're talking about seem inconsequential in the grand scheme of the universe. Anything that affects our hearts is important to God.

Prayer Is a Reminder to Us that God Is Wise Beyond Our Understanding

Sometimes we act like our prayers are a formula. Instead of having a conversation with God, we might pray in an attempt to get him to do the things we want. It's as though we think if we pray a certain way or use specific words, we'll eventually find the combination to release our deepest desires from God's hands.

The truth is, God gives according to his wisdom, in light of all he knows of eternity and our lives. It's not because we've said the right things or asked him for something a certain number of times. As God's children, we can always ask him for anything without shame. And when God chooses to answer our prayers differently than we want, it's an opportunity for us to choose trust in him over trust in our circumstances.

Prayer Is More than a Wish List

While we're always welcome to ask our Father, who cares for the desires of our heart, for things we deeply need, there's so much more we can carry to God when we pray. When we've sinned, we can talk about it with God, who already wiped it away once we asked for forgiveness. We can use prayer to tell God how much we love him, how grateful we are for who he is and all he does for us, and how thankful we are for his presence in our life. And sometimes we may simply talk the way we would with our best friends, discussing our happiness or our heartache.

Prayer Is an Opportunity to Be Intentional About Listening to God.

It's important for us to listen to what *God* wants to tell us when we pray. God speaks to us all the time: through Scripture, through the Holy Spirit's nudging, through those who are close to him, and through certain circumstances in our lives. Prayer is a way we can keep the conversation from being one-sided, and it's another way we can be active participants in our faith as followers of Jesus.

The psalmist in Psalm 17 says that when we pray, God listens. Imagine God leaning toward you, tilting his head and giving you his full attention. He's delighted when we come to him, whether we're telling him about a new passion we've discovered or we're upset over a situation that seems completely unfair.

He never runs out of time to get things done or is too busy to hear what we've got on our hearts. His heart is full of love and longing for us. He has all of eternity to listen to what we have to say.

Live

How do you usually pray? Do you have conversations with God like you have conversations with a close friend? If your prayers sound more like a birthday wish list than a heart-to-heart, there's no need to beat yourself up over it. God still enjoys hearing from you, but his desire is for you to share everything with him, not just the things you long for. Today, make connecting with God the priority in your prayer.

Pray

Dear Lord, thank you for hearing me. I'm grateful you love me so much that you want me to spend time with you and have a conversation with you, even though you're powerful and holy and need nothing. My heart is all I have to offer, and I know you love my heart. Please help me value our relationship over anything else.

Think

God designed prayer to be a special connection between him and me, a reminder of his infinite power and his love for me.

God's Heart for Freedom

The Spirit of the Sovereign LORD is on me, because the LORD has anointed me to proclaim good news to the poor. He has sent me to bind up the brokenhearted, to proclaim freedom for the captives and release from darkness for the prisoners.

ISAIAH 61:1

ots of people know about the Ten Commandments. Maybe they've seen them while passing through a courtroom lobby, or perhaps they've taken notice when someone quotes one on a picket sign. It seems the Ten Commandments are *all* some people know about the Bible, and many people aren't fond of having a bunch of rules to follow.

There aren't many of us who enjoy being told what to do. If we aren't in relationship with Jesus, we might read the Bible and start believing its main purpose is to make us prisoners to a bunch of outdated rules. If we take that approach, we miss the fact that the Bible is actually a book about freedom. Our freedom.

Focusing only on rules can be a prison. And when we find ourselves believing the rules are what save us, they can absolutely become bondage instead of freedom—something that we need to be constrained by. Or we might think we're free simply because we're following the rules. *True* freedom comes from knowing that what we do isn't what saves us. God has already done the work of saving our hearts by sending us Jesus. Following rules because we believe it will make God love us more is a prison of our own making.

Completely ignoring God's rules can also be a prison. Getting stuck on what we *can't* do is one of Satan's oldest tricks. In the garden of Eden, Satan not only called attention to what God had asked Eve not to do, he twisted what God really said, and he made it sound like she was imprisoned by the single rule God had given—a rule that protected her pure, unlimited freedom. When Eve—and then Adam—broke that rule, everything became bondage. They lost their freedoms, and ours, by choosing to go against the best God had set out for them from the beginning.

Rules aren't the only things we find ourselves imprisoned by, either. Sometimes we find ourselves locked in the prison cells of our past, made of the difficult or downright terrible things we've experienced. When others break our hearts by acting in unloving ways, it's easy to hunker down in the corner of a prison cell we've built with bricks of hurt, unforgiveness, anger, and bitterness. If we're not careful, we can live in that place for the rest of our lives, holding on to those damaging feelings.

It's not that we're not supposed to feel anything negative when we're wronged by other people—it's just that we can't stay there and live in that place indefinitely. We can't camp out in our pain. We have to move through it.

Dealing with these feelings matters. It isn't easy and often hurts, but we're never alone, even as we process the hard things in our lives. Jesus cares about what we've been through, and he cares about our freedom. If we hold on to the hurt we've experienced, elevating it above and beyond what God offers, we remain imprisoned.

God wants us to be have freedom. He's offered us a key, one that unlocks the gates of every prison we'll ever be in, and that key is the true gospel—the good news of Jesus' pursuit and rescue of each of our hearts. Jesus' sacrifice gives the promise of release to every one of us. Those of us who have been released have a responsibility to go out on his behalf, sharing the truth of his heart for freedom and rescue with others, so they too can find release from their personal prisons.

Not that sharing that message of freedom is always easy. If someone else's prison reminds us of our own, or if we're unfamiliar with the things keeping them in bondage, we might turn to our fear or discomfort instead of acting with hearts full of freedom and boldness. But when we've asked Jesus to be the Lord of our lives, we have God's fearless, powerful spirit in us. We can't encounter bondage and do nothing. Leading others toward rescue is part of our calling.

When Jesus walked the earth, he constantly offered freedom to those stuck in their own prisons. Some of them were chained up by bad decisions from their past, like Zacchaeus the tax collector. (To whom Jesus said, "Come down immediately. I must stay at your house today.") Others were bound by things they had no control over, like the woman who had been bleeding for twelve years. (To whom Jesus said, "Go in peace and be freed from your suffering.") And when the teachers of the law couldn't see the prisons others were trapped in because of their own imprisonment to the law, Jesus told them the parable of the good shepherd.

Following our Savior's example, we're to rush toward those who are imprisoned, extending freedom and showing them the way to true liberty, the way to Jesus. We rush toward them with abandon, joyfully sharing the details of our freedom.

Freedom isn't for a few people who are lucky enough to figure things out for themselves. Freedom is for everyone!

Live

Where do you find yourself imprisoned today? Are you ready to leave your imprisonment behind? Ask God to open your eyes to the ways you cling to captivity instead of embracing and living in the freedom he offers.

Pray

Dear Lord, there's absolutely nothing I can do on my own to drag myself out of the prisons I find myself in. But I trust you and believe you offer me freedom. Help me walk in the freedom you give me. Show me the steps I need to take to leave my captivity behind. I want a life of glorious freedom, and I want to share that with others. Thank you for making freedom possible for me. Keep my heart open and aware of opportunities to share the freedom I have in Jesus with everyone else I encounter.

Think

God wants me to have freedom, and he's stopped at nothing to make sure I have every opportunity to walk in it.

PART THREE

A Heart for Others

The Greatest News of All Time

This is how we know what love is: Jesus Christ laid down his life for us. And we ought to lay down our lives for our brothers and sisters. If anyone has material possessions and sees a brother or sister in need but has no pity on them, how can the love of God be in that person? Dear children, let us not love with words or speech but with actions and in truth.

This is how we know that we belong to the truth and how we set our hearts at rest in his presence: If our hearts condemn us, we know that God is greater than our hearts, and he knows everything.

1 JOHN 3:16–20

Any time we're in a relationship with someone, there are signs that point to the existence of that relationship. If the relationship is with a boyfriend, we might keep mementos from dates, like movie ticket stubs and dried-up flowers in a dresser drawer. We'll smile when we talk about him.

People can usually guess which people are our best friends because we start to have the same mannerisms after spending lots of time together. We share inside jokes and lots of memories and books full of pictures together. That kind of relationship is hard to cover up.

A relationship with Jesus is no different. When we're walking with Jesus, there are "mementos" we collect along the way, reminders of the experiences we've had with him. Whole-hearted Christ followers exhibit signs of their relationship with him, indicators that clue others in to the presence of their faith journeys.

Our faith can be very internally focused if we let it stay that way. It's easy to say that your walk with Jesus is *only* between you and Jesus. It's true nobody else can make the choice to follow Jesus for us—it's a decision that is ours and ours alone. But when our faith is real and when our relationship with Jesus has changed us, there's evidence in the way we live our lives. Our faith isn't meant to be hidden. It's meant to be shared.

We might be tempted to say the "signs" of a thriving relationship with Jesus are things like raising our hands when the worship team sings our favorite song, or making sure others know we don't approve of their sin, but that doesn't necessarily line up with what Scripture tells us.

First John 3:16–18 reminds us to "not love with words or speech but with actions and in truth." The evidence of our love for Jesus is in the way we choose to lay down our lives for our brothers and sisters here on earth.

It sounds super intense and very scary, doesn't it? Laying down our lives is a incredibly big ask, an enormous requirement that doesn't come naturally to any of us. And yet, it's what Jesus did for us. He's the only one who could have died to make things right between us and God.

For us, however, we may not need to lay down our literal lives. Instead, it may be that we have to make daily decisions to lay down our desires and our comfort as signs of our relationships with Jesus. Or make personal sacrifices that will help point others to Jesus.

Love isn't only for when the gestures are sweeping and the audience before us is large. Those opportunities to show love are exciting, and we should act when we recognize them. But the majority of the time the signs of love and our relationships with Jesus feel smaller and more mundane.

It may not seem like an act of love to clean toilets or to share a message of hope when three people show up to hear it, but quiet actions of a heart that's following Jesus are just as loud with love as the grand announcements and enormous events.

God often does things in ways that seem backward to us since we look at them through eyes that can't see the big picture in the same way he does. But God lets nothing go to waste. Even if the things we're doing seem pointless or useless, we can be confident that God is still at work. We are where we are for his purposes, and he gives us opportunities to love and lay down our lives all the time.

It's not easy or insignificant to embrace things that feel like inconveniences and choose to see them as opportunities instead, but this is how we lay down our lives in service to Jesus. Following Jesus' example of laying down his life and loving others well will make a difference. Others take notice because it's such a foreign, seemingly backward way to live in a world that's bent on making a big deal out of ourselves. When we serve others out of a heart in love with Jesus, the rest of the world changes. And so do we.

In the kingdom of God, we are saved by the fact Jesus laid down his life for us to save the world. As his followers, we daily lay down our lives to serve the world and share his love with everyone who needs it. Only God could use something as dark and painful as death to give us life. Only God takes our offering of lives laid down in service and love, no matter how small and mundane or grand and sweeping, and uses it to make his love for us, and for the whole world, loud.

Live

How have you experienced a life laid down for you? Can you remember an instance when someone in your life made sacrifices to show you Jesus' love? Where do you think you can begin to lay down your life so others can see his love too?

Pray

Dear Jesus, I know it's important to love others well, and I want to do this more in my life. When I come up against a choice to lay down my life in service to someone or to walk away, remind me of how you will meet me in the laying down. Remind me of how the world and my heart can be changed by my choice to serve you.

Think

A heart that loves others well is always on the lookout for the big and little opportunities to serve and make God's love loud.

Being Trustworthy in the "Little Things"

"Whoever can be trusted with very little can also be trusted with much, and whoever is dishonest with very little will also be dishonest with much. So if you have not been trustworthy in handling worldly wealth, who will trust you with true riches? And if you have not been trustworthy with someone else's property, who will give you property of your own?"

LUKE 16:10–12

If you were to invest money, you'd have to review the minimum requirements for that type of account. All banks and investment firms require something to begin the process. If we invest nothing at the bank, we get nothing in return. We all understand that multiplying zero, no matter how many times it's multiplied, will always result in nothing. And that if we put in an initial investment—even if it is small—the process of interest and monetary growth can begin, and there will be something in the bank to withdraw later when we need it.

But in life, we sometimes convince ourselves that if we can't do big things right away, we shouldn't do anything at all. We feel ashamed of our starting places because of how they compare to where other people already are. Can you imagine if this was how God saw our lives? We never would have begun in the first place if he didn't intend for there to be a journey of growing and becoming.

We start out small, depending on our parents to care for us

and teach us. Now we largely care for ourselves, but there was a time when these actions weren't second nature to us. There's also a moment when we hear the Word of God for the first time and it settles like a seedling into our hearts. Over time, God helps it to grow. The longer we follow him and seek his heart, the more we mature and the more we become like Jesus. But there's always a beginning.

We're each unique, and we all have a specific, only-us story. The gifts we've been given, the dreams we carry in our hearts, and the people and causes we're passionate about are all in place because God set them in our hearts, in hopes we'd discover them and they would draw us nearer to him. It's our responsibility to take notice of the distinct pieces of our identity that God has given us as his daughters. Then we must tend to and nurture those things even when they're still small beginnings.

Anything we do with a heart dedicated to serving God has enormous purpose. He has a direct view into our hearts, and it's pleasing to him when we freely give what we have. Nothing is little when we act out of a pure heart that wants to make God's name great. We may have visions of doing big things for many people, and that vision may match up with what God has planned for our lives in the years to come, but we have to tend and nurture what's in front of us right now.

It isn't a formula to get what we want out of our lives, though. There is no guarantee that if we speak to a group of three that we'll be granted an audience of thousands in the future, even if we're faithful with what God's given us now. Expecting more because of our performance isn't the point.

The *more* of what God has in store for us is that we become *more* like Jesus. When we seek more for ourselves, it leads to a disordered heart that's obsessed with our own image and making ourselves into a big deal. But when we're committed to becoming more like Jesus and making him a big deal, any additional blessings we receive are just like icing on the top of the cupcake. It's *wonderful*, but it's extra.

We may never know the impact of our lives, even when we live them in dedication to loving and serving Jesus. There may never be a big stage or a massive, sparkly dream come true. But we know the One who has put us where we are, the One who's chosen to give us what we already have. He's put us where we are for his purposes, and we can trust that he's done the preparation and work inside of us for our good and for his best.

It's tempting to look at the stories others live out and to lust after what they have or be envious of their lifestyles. But God gave their stories to them with the same care and purpose as the stories he's given to us. We don't need to grab and scramble for the return others have received on what they've invested because we have our own investments to manage and tend.

This also serves as a reminder to extend extra grace to other people we meet and know. They may still be tending their small beginnings, learning and growing and trying to figure out what it looks like to live with their gifts and passions. It's not easy to begin, it's not easy to be in the middle, and it's not easy to finish. So wherever another person is in the investment process of his or her life, have grace and pour kindness out over them. Maybe that kindness is what's needed to help them grow.

God has been faithful to give us everything we need for life and godliness (see 2 Peter 1:3 for more on this). Nothing God does is wasted, and nothing he asks us to do is worthless, even if it seems small and insignificant.

Though we may not understand his purposes now, we can trust that he sees the fullness of the big picture of our lives. His plans are good and necessary. Because we trust his heart for us, we can trust that we're doing what's necessary, even if that necessary looks tiny and frail. It's a beginning, and the way we tend our beginnings helps us have good habits we'll need to continue growing and becoming more like Jesus across our entire lives.

Live

What small beginnings do you see in your life? How do you feel about these beginnings? Spend time thinking about the dreams you carry in your heart. Ask God how you can be faithful with what you have right now, and ask him to make you excited by the journey of becoming who he intends you to become over time, and the investments you can make for God's kingdom along the way.

Pray

Dear Lord, I confess that sometimes I feel jealous and anxious about the gifts other people have and what their lives look like. It seems like they have more opportunity and more resources to reach their dreams than I do. But I trust that you've given me everything I need, and I trust that you've placed me where I am because you see the big picture of my life and how I fit into eternity. Would you help me find peace within the process you have planned for me? I'd rather be like you instead of being a big deal for the sake of being a big deal. Remind me of my journey whenever I start to forget.

Think

A person with a heart for others trusts that her small beginnings aren't meaningless, no matter how small they can feel.

When Faith and Works Collide

What good is it, my brothers and sisters, if someone claims to have faith but has no deeds? Can such faith save them? Suppose a brother or a sister is without clothes and daily food. If one of you says to them, "Go in peace; keep warm and well fed," but does nothing about their physical needs, what good is it? In the same way, faith by itself, if it is not accompanied by action, is dead.

JAMES 2:14–17

One of the go-to conversation starters we all fall back on is the topic of our passions, the things we love to do and the activities we enjoy more than anything else. What if, when you met a new friend and you asked about her passions, she said, "I'm so glad you asked. I *love* basketball. It's my favorite sport of all time. I can't stop thinking about basketball. I even dream about it all night long. I have the most amazing collection of basketballs and basketball shoes and basketball playbooks."

Naturally, you'd follow up by asking her about this passion of hers. What position does she like to play? How long has she been playing? What's her favorite basketball team?

You'd expect her to have quick answers to these questions and a few fun stories to share since she's just proclaimed herself to be an enormous basketball fanatic.

But what if she looked at you and shrugged? What if she

said, "Oh, I love the sport. But I don't play. I don't even watch the game."

Everything she just told you would be completely void. You'd feel incredibly confused, and you might even wonder if she's able to tell the truth or if she just says what sounds good in the moment.

There's no way she could be as big of a fan as she says if she doesn't participate in the game at all. Her words sounded authentic at first, but her actions and the way she lives her life reveal her reality.

This is sort of what it's like when we say we're Christ followers but we choose not to live a life of love and freedom. Other people hear what we say, though when they find out we hate people who are different from us or that we aren't willing to help our neighbors, they are utterly confused.

We don't have to do good things or have a lifestyle centered on kindness to earn a spot for ourselves in heaven. There's nothing we could do that's good enough or kind enough to earn us even a chance of getting there on our own, so that's why we're so grateful for Jesus. He took care of that for us.

But when we say we follow Christ, part of that means we want to be like him. When we read the Gospels (Matthew, Mark, Luke, and John), we see how Jesus lived a life full of actions that matched up with the words he spoke.

He came to give everyone on earth freedom. It's our calling to continue showing others how they can have that freedom. If we can do something to make the freedom Jesus offers tangible to, or able to be experienced by, other people, why wouldn't we do it?

We aren't saved because of what we do, but what we do is in response to the fact we've been rescued. Our hearts show themselves through our actions. When we've encountered God and come face-to-face with his mercy, that experience becomes the fuel for what we do in response. We can't help but act.

Sometimes we're tempted to turn the other way when we see opportunities to serve someone else. It's uncomfortable. We don't want to make the sacrifice. We're afraid of looking stupid or we're just plain afraid. We don't want to be identified as "one of them," or we don't want other people to think we're supportive of sin. Whatever our reasons for not serving someone else, they all fall away when we hold them up to the example of Jesus.

Being uncomfortable isn't going to damage us for life. In fact, when we leave our comfort zones, it adds extra energy and vibrancy to our faith journeys.

When we sacrifice for others, we grow beyond what we thought we'd be able to handle. Sacrifice reminds us of all we already have and all that we can be grateful for. Our fear of helping others reveals where our trust really lies and where we have room to grow. When we serve and love people who believe differently than we do or who act differently than we act, it helps us to become more empathetic. The issues we've only talked about before suddenly have names and faces.

Proverbs 3:27 says, "Do not withhold good from those to whom it is due, when it is in your power to act." As Christ followers, we have access to the power that raised Jesus from the dead, so no excuses there. And we know the source of the greatest good that will ever exist!

This is so exciting. There's no shortage of opportunities to love and serve no matter where we are in life. Our homes, our churches, our communities, and our entire planet are full of people who need to know about the great lengths Jesus went to so he could gift them with freedom.

How gracious is God to remind us of the freedom and love he's given to us when we step out to share that freedom and love with other people? We serve and do good because our hearts are overflowing with the love he's shown us. And then on top of that love, he continues to fill our hearts and help us become more like him.

Only things that have died or things that were never alive to begin with do nothing. We're alive, and our hearts are alive with the love of Christ! Let's share that love whenever and however we can.

Live

Think about your home, your church, your community, and the entire world. Is there a way you can share the freedom of Christ in each of these environments? What can you do today to put God's love on display in your life?

Pray

Dear Jesus, I'm excited by the idea that I can show other people who you are by the way I reflect your love. Whenever I have the opportunity to love someone, would you nudge me to do that? Would you help me to recognize when I'm making excuses and give me the courage to love anyway? My relationship with you is important to me, and I want other people to be able to see that through the way I act. Help me to be obedient to you, and help me to be an excellent representative of your kingdom by acting out of a heart filled with your love and freedom.

Think

A heart that loves others can't help but share the freedom and love of Jesus with the rest of the world by taking action.

Having a Light-Heart

"You are the light of the world. A town built on a hill cannot be hidden. Neither do people light a lamp and put it under a bowl. Instead they put it on its stand, and it gives light to everyone in the house. In the same way, let your light shine before others, that they may see your good deeds and glorify your Father in heaven."

MATTHEW 5:14–16

On Christmas Eve, many churches have a candlelight service. The lights inside are turned off in preparation, and the sanctuary plunges into darkness. For a heavy moment, all is still and light is gone. Then one person strikes a match. Everyone sees something again, even if it's only the single light.

The darkness still exists, but the one flame has already become a beacon to all, a foreshadowing of what's to come.

A person in the front row touches her candle to the match, and the darkness shrinks again. She shares the light with her neighbor, who shares it with his neighbor, who shares it with a person in the row behind them. In a short amount of time, faces reappear, illuminated by the candlelight. Soon the darkness is gone, and the light takes over.

All it took to bring light to the darkness was a single flame and someone with a willingness to share. One flame chases away darkness. Lots of candles together obliterate it.

Remember what Jesus said in John 8:12: He is the light of the world. If you follow him, you will never walk in darkness. Instead, you carry light in your heart everywhere you go.

Now reread Matthew 5:14–16. You too are the light of the world. And Jesus wants you to "let your light shine before others, that they may see your good deeds and glorify your Father in heaven."

Light is one of the most necessary resources we have. God created the light before anything else came into existence. It shines in front of us so we know where to walk and it helps us avoid the dangers that lurk in darkness. Light feeds plants and plankton and keeps the earth flourishing. It provides warmth. Light reveals things that were hidden. We simply can't survive, much less grow and thrive, without light in our lives.

What if, on Christmas Eve, the first person with the flame took her light and immediately rushed to stuff it underneath an empty coffee cup? We'd know something was wrong. Nobody lights a candle only to hide it seconds later. That would completely negate the purpose of the candle.

We, as followers of Jesus, have light-hearts—hearts that are radiant with his light. It's as though we're carrying lit candles in a world where the lights have been turned out. Sharing the light of Jesus is the purpose of our lives. If we stifle his light by choosing to live in sin and shame, we cancel out our truest purpose and our greatest calling.

Putting Christ's light on display in our lives isn't like pulling out a spotlight and shining it into others' eyes to force them into relationship with Jesus. And it's certainly not turning that spotlight back onto ourselves. We just have to shine out what we have.

Having a light-heart is simple, but that doesn't mean it's easy. Serving our neighbors or loving people who believe differently from us isn't comfortable and it isn't something many of us do naturally. Putting real truth and love on display is difficult, especially when other people seem to believe truth and love are irrelevant and nonexistent.

Sometimes we might feel afraid or unworthy to talk about Jesus with other people because we're scared we might say the wrong things or do something that would push others away. But sharing Jesus is about him, not us, and the rest of the world needs him as much as we do. Jesus is all we have to offer, and he's who people need to hear and see in our lives.

When we fix our eyes on Jesus, we do these things out of our love for him. A lot of people may be unwilling to pick up a Bible to read about Jesus, and you probably have friends who've told you they aren't interested in stepping into a church. But it's hard to turn away from the light of Jesus when they truly see it in another person. Nobody would ignore a flashlight in a cave if they were in danger. When people encounter the light of Jesus in our lives, they will take notice, even if they aren't receptive to his rescue yet.

So love Jesus and love others well! Let the light of Christ shine brightly through you. Allow him to become irresistible to the people you know by uncovering your light-heart and letting the light of Christ obliterate the darkness everywhere else. The Giver of Light has provided us with everything we need to share his light. Now we can remind others exactly how much he loves them and wants to give them life to the fullest extent. Jesus is on a rescue mission, and we get to be a part of it.

The single match on Christmas Eve doesn't seem like much at first. But if that flame were hidden or it wasn't shared with anybody else, the sanctuary would remain in the dark. We might convince ourselves it's not much to listen to a friend who's having a bad week or to take crackers and Sprite to our neighbor with a stomach bug, but God can use anything to show off his light. We can't hide from the opportunities to share our light-hearts or refuse to be Jesus to hurting people. The darkness doesn't deserve to stay any longer than it already has.

Let your light-heart shine, and may the darkness be obliterated.

Live

Are you tempted to cover your light-heart at times? What circumstances tempt you to hide your relationship with Jesus? What can you do today to let his light shine brighter through you?

Pray

Jesus, I'm glad you're the source of light and truth. I know I don't get everything right, and sometimes I come across as being unloving or as a poor representation of your heart. Would you point out the ways I may be covering up my light-heart? Help me to be a bright and loving reflection of you when I'm around other people so they'll recognize that you're reaching out to rescue them.

Think

A Christ follower is always on the lookout for ways to let her light-heart shine bright so others will want to know more about the Source of her light.

Reaching for the Outsider

When a Samaritan woman came to draw water, Jesus said to her, "Will you give me a drink?" (His disciples had gone into the town to buy food.)

The Samaritan woman said to him, "You are a Jew and I am a Samaritan woman. How can you ask me for a drink?" (For Jews do not associate with Samaritans.)

Jesus answered her, "If you knew the gift of God and who it is that asks you for a drink, you would have asked him and he would have given you living water."

JOHN 4:7-10

Have you ever felt as though you were an outsider? Maybe you started at a new school in February, after all the other students were well past getting to know each other and already knew where to sit in the cafeteria and who their chemistry partners were.

Or maybe you're the one who's been going to school with the same people since pre-K. You know the seating routine in the cafeteria, and your best friend is always your chemistry partner. But still, your heart feels lonely sometimes because in your family, you feel like you've been forgotten.

The truth is, we've all felt left out and lonely before, because that's real life. We even have an acronym for feeling like we're on the outside looking in: FOMO, or the Fear of Missing Out. It's that sinking feeling that settles heavy in your stomach when your friends go out for ice cream but you have to stay behind to write an essay, or when your cousins spend a week at the beach without you. Whether we were left out intentionally or accidentally, we all likely have a story to share. We all hurt when we're left behind.

Jesus knows all about how it feels to be lonely and out of place. He didn't seem to belong anywhere, being born to a teen mom and a carpenter while they were traveling, not while they were safe at home. His siblings weren't all that excited to be his siblings. When he was a kid, he went to the temple and began teaching. (Do you think that made him very popular with the other kids his age?) In Matthew 8:20, he says that even though the animals on earth have homes, "the Son of Man has no place to lay his head."

But he also had the best "in" of all eternity. As the Son of God, Jesus knew his belonging on earth didn't matter nearly as much as his forever in eternity with his Father. Though on earth he may have been considered an outsider, he is the reason the rest of us have access to the best family of all time, the family of believers who call God our Father as well.

Many of the stories in the Gospels show how Jesus made it a practice in his life to move toward the ones everyone else considered to be "on the outside."

One of the "outsiders" Jesus included was the Samaritan woman at the well. She had gone to get water at noon (the hottest part of the day when no one else trekked to the well) to avoid the shame surrounding her many marriages and current boyfriend situation, and she met the man who showed her that he is Living Water. Jesus spoke to her as she came near. Culturally, it wasn't something anyone would have considered acceptable. The Jews and the Samaritans, as the Bible notes, didn't associate with each other. Men and women who weren't married weren't supposed to hang out in public together, either.

What mattered to Jesus, though, was that the woman who needed water needed even more to be introduced to the Father, so he introduced himself. He asked her for a drink, and then told her how the thirst in her soul could be quenched. She hadn't told him about her many husbands and the boyfriend she was currently living with, but Jesus knew it anyway and called it out. Her behavior may as well have been salt water. Salt water, to a thirsty person, only makes them thirstier.

Because of the way she'd chosen to live her life and because of her gender and because of her ethnicity, this was a woman well acquainted with life on the fringes. But Jesus wasn't afraid of her and he wasn't afraid of what it would look like if he talked to her. So he invited her into communion with himself. He knew he could offer to her what she needed the most, so he did. Jesus moved toward her.

Sometimes we hesitate to step closer to people we see as outsiders, and we separate ourselves from them instead. What are we afraid of? Maybe that others will see our proximity to them and think less of us? Or are we scared we'll get dragged into the sins they struggle with?

Anything that keeps us from sharing the gospel with people who need it is bogus. It's fake! It's the salt water of excuses that will never satisfy. We may avoid temporary discomfort or gossip along the way, but we'll know in our hearts we could have (and should have!) done something.

Those of us who know God as our Father belong to the best family of all time, and because we've been welcomed into this family we should reach for those who haven't been adopted yet.

Sometimes we expect our churches or missionaries to do all the reaching. They're the ones who trained to do that stuff, right? It may be their job, but we're all equally called to reach out and offer the news of who Jesus is and what he did for us.

Sitting in our rows at church every Sunday and waiting for the outsiders to step inside isn't enough. We're the ones who've already become family, the ones who know Jesus as the answer to our deepest need, the ones on the inside.

It's our responsibility to reach for those on the outside.

Live

Have you noticed anyone in your life who seems to hang out on the fringes? Have you avoided someone because of fear? Make it a point to pursue people who need Jesus today. Start up a conversation. Be their friend. Reach for them.

Pray

Dear Lord, I want to help as many people know you as I can. I'm grateful to be your daughter. I know the people around me who don't know you have a hunger to be in relationship with you, even if they might not know how to reach you or even that you are the one who can truly fill them. Open my eyes to the opportunities I have to reach for them, to show them they belong in our family.

Thank you for loving me and drawing near to me when I still had no clue how much I needed you. You're the greatest fulfillment of every prayer I've ever prayed and everything my heart has ever needed.

Think

A Christ follower doesn't accept excuses when it comes to her ability to reach people who need Jesus and are looking for a place to belong.

Loving My Non-Christian Friends

But thanks be to God, who always leads us as captives in Christ's triumphal procession and uses us to spread the aroma of the knowledge of him everywhere. For we are to God the pleasing aroma of Christ among those who are being saved and those who are perishing. To the one we are an aroma that brings death; to the other, an aroma that brings life. And who is equal to such a task? Unlike so many, we do not peddle the word of God for profit. On the contrary, in Christ we speak before God with sincerity, as those sent from God.

2 CORINTHIANS 2:14–17

The smell of an excellent breakfast has great power.

It can beckon you back to a sweet memory of your grandmother making biscuits and sausage gravy for you in the morning after you'd spent the night at her house. A whiff of a cup of hot tea and a buttery croissant might help you get going in the morning. Even those of us who aren't morning people may be lured out from under the covers by the smell of cinnamon rolls baking in the oven.

The fragrance of breakfast calls us to something, whether it's an old memory or new anticipation, wakefulness or comfort. Our bodies even respond with a rumbling stomach or a watering mouth. The smell of breakfast food always invokes a response.

As followers of Jesus, we also have a fragrance, an essence

that exudes from our hearts and spirits that others notice when we spend time together and grow in friendship with them. Second Corinthians 2 says that as believers, to God we carry the pleasing fragrance of Christ. Since Christ stepped in and became our substitute, God experiences the essence of Jesus every time we come near to him.

If we're around our nonbelieving friends and they think the main focus of a relationship with Jesus is the fact they are sinners and "unworthy," they're missing out on the whole story. To them the "aroma" is an aroma of death because that's what sin is. But when they really encounter Jesus, they experience the full fragrance, the aroma of life as we experience it as believers.

When we hang out with friends who don't know Jesus yet, we want to help them encounter the aroma of Christ instead of continually pointing out the aroma of sin and death. While it's true that sin exists in all our lives, it's hard to convince someone of how much they're loved when the focus is on how much they do wrong.

Once our friends encounter Jesus for real, they'll recognize all the right stuff because of the work of God in their hearts. But they aren't there yet if they don't know him!

If we're super hungry and we smell the aroma of a nearby restaurant or someone slow-roasting barbecue, it makes our mouths water. The way we live out our love for Jesus should be that mouth-watering aroma to our friends who don't believe yet. It isn't what we preach to our friends, it's what we practice that helps them smell the fragrance of life and freedom. It might feel like we're doing nothing if we're not calling out sin all the time, but that's not true. Just living a life as an authentic, kind, and loving woman in relationship with Jesus says a lot!

We do this by sharing our real lives with everyone, and that includes our friends who don't believe. The true and authentic daily stuff everybody experiences, and how we handle those things, makes a bigger impression than any sanitized, tidied-up version we try to pass off as real. That's because even Christ followers go through really tough times. We might think we're "protecting God's reputation" if we share only the great things in our lives, but that's not an honest representation of what life looks like when we walk with Jesus. If we convince people that a relationship with Jesus is always spic-and-span, nothing but sunshine and sparkles, then they'll question their new faith journey the second difficulty shows up.

Lots of people wonder if God is still good even though bad things still happen. That's not a new question, even for our friends who don't follow Jesus yet. So we don't need to pretend like following Jesus somehow looks more attractive when we hide the hard stuff. He's present and real even in the middle of the tough times. And people need to see that so they know the support and comfort Jesus can offer, and can learn to go to Jesus when they struggle.

Show your friends what it looks like when a Christ follower focuses on forgiveness and repentance instead of giving in to guilt when she messes up. Let them see how you rely on Jesus even in the middle of crushing disappointment. Be honest about how it feels when you don't have all the answers or feel confused about tragedy or injustice, and show them how God gives us the freedom to ask him about these things. When we're authentic and honest about our faith in Jesus, it helps our friends feel free to be authentic and honest about their questions and experiences about him.

One caution: Sometimes when we have friends who aren't believers yet, we might get wrapped up in making sure our friends are "converted." When we do this, it can lead to treating them as causes instead of as our friends. We'll know we've fallen into this trap if our hearts react with overwhelming despair when our friends show no interest in having conversations about Jesus, or we feel angry when they refuse our invitations to church events. We could be tempted to walk away when their behavior remains unchanged, even after months of our prayers.

Truthfully, these can be symptoms of our own puffed-up-ness instead of real love for our friends. Those behaviors reveal the less-than-lovely reality that we've relegated our friends to a checklist in our hearts, the checklist we've secretly convinced ourselves earns us extra points with God. But friendship isn't a game or a challenge or a means to an end.

We don't pretend to love our friends who don't know Jesus yet because it looks good on our "Christian résumés." We love them because they're people who carry his image and deserve to be loved just like we do. So when you notice your heart tilting toward achievement instead of affection for your friends, leave that behavior behind and love your friends with the love of Jesus, whether they know him or not.

Our friends may not choose to step into relationship with Jesus during the course of our friendships with them. We don't know the big picture of their lives and what God has in store for them. Our friendship may be the starting point of their faith journeys and not the turning point.

Friendship is an enormous gift, and this is also true of our friendships with people who don't know Jesus yet. Live your life with love and authenticity—let the fragrance of Christ be bold and as beautiful to your friends who don't believe yet as the smell of breakfast is to a starving person.

Live

Which of your friends aren't believers? What characterizes your relationship with them? Do you think they feel preached at or do you think they're able to smell the natural fragrance of Christ in your life? Take a few minutes to reflect on how you treat those friends and how your heart feels when they don't seem interested in matters of faith.

Pray

Dear Jesus, I want my friend (use her name!) to know you and be in relationship with you. I know you want the same thing. When I hang out with her, help her to see that you're real and actively involved in my life. Help me to have the aroma of life, and let that be appealing to her. Remind me to always love my friend for who she is, a woman made in the image of Christ, instead of focusing only on the challenge of her spirituality.

Think

A person with a heart for others loves people for who they are now and lives authentically so her friends are encouraged by the aroma of Jesus in her life.

We Need Heart Friends

Walk with the wise and become wise, for a companion of fools suffers harm.

PROVERBS 13:20

Anne Shirley arrived at Green Gables with little other than the *e* on the end of her name. No food. No family. And certainly no friends. If you've read *Anne of Green Gables*, or if you've seen the movies or TV series, you know things don't stay that way for long, because nearly everyone in the story falls in love with the orphaned girl with carrot-colored braids.

One of the most important moments in Anne's life was the moment she met her best friend, kindred spirit Diana Barry. Their friendship started when they were children and continued throughout their lifetimes. Anne and Diana were heart friends: women who saw each other's hearts, knew their depths, and loved each other because of and despite what was there in those hearts.

Maybe you have a friend like this, a kindred spirit who shares the best and worst moments of your life with you. Or maybe you think a friendship like that can only be a work of fiction because none of your friendships (if you could even call them that) come close.

It's true that heart-melding, soul-knowing, be-there-no-matter-what friendships don't happen all the time. But all that means is when you *do* find the heart-melding, soul-knowing, be-there-no-matter-what types of friends, you hold on and love well. Real, honest friendship is even for those of us who were so sick of being betrayed, hurt, and lied to that we decided a long time ago not to depend on anybody.

Friendship changes us. Good, godly friendship changes our hearts, our minds, and our stories for the better. Proverbs 13:20 is an excellent reminder of how we start to take on the characteristics of the people we spend the most time with, so it's important to choose our closest friends wisely.

If we want to learn how to be good students, we sit next to the smartest kid in our class. We watch the way she takes notes. We pay attention to the kind of questions she asks. We study with her and do homework in study hall the way she does. At the end of the semester, we're likely better at studying, better with time management, and better students overall simply because we paid attention to someone else who did those things well.

People don't wear signs that say "I'm a great friend!" though, so how do we know who we should choose to stick with and who we should choose not to allow in our lives as influencers?

We pay attention. Remember how Matthew 7 talks about good trees bearing good fruit and bad trees bearing bad fruit? Whatever we embrace in our hearts eventually makes its way into our lives as visible fruit. So when considering a new friend, watch for their fruit.

A heart friend will remind us of our true identity when we've started to forget. She tells us, and keeps telling us, who we really are as daughters of the Living God. There aren't belittling or backhanded compliments. A heart friend—the kind of woman who's worth letting in and holding on to—is a person who wants to see you fully alive, and she's there to cheer you on the whole way. When your dreams seem impossible and your heart feels withered up, she's the kind of person who goes out of her way to remind you this isn't the end of your story and that your identity is safe and secure in Jesus.

A heart friend will call out the junk in our lives and remind us to run after better things. Heart friends aren't going to slap some eyeshadow and lip gloss on your sin and call it pretty. They're going to risk hurting your feelings for a moment to keep you from waking up a decade from now so far from Jesus that you're not sure you'd even recognize his name anymore.

A heart friend will speak the truth when all we seem to hear are lies. Bullies exist. Nobody has to remind us of this because we've all likely faced that behavior at some point. Most bullies are easy to point out because we can see their faces and recognize their voices. But what about when we bully ourselves? We sometimes let those moments slide. But a heart friend will call us out when we speak lies over our own hearts instead of singing life to ourselves.

A heart friend shows up when we're happy. She's ready to celebrate. Your dream came true? She's tossing confetti. You had the best day ever? She's grabbing ice cream with you to celebrate. Whatever it is, a true friend scatters extra joy sprinkles on top of your good news because she loves it for you. There's no grasping to take credit for something you've done or knocking you down so she can reach a milestone first. She's genuinely your fan, and she makes your joy-filled times better.

A heart friend shows up when we're sad. If a friend *only* came around when things were good, we'd have a right to be skeptical, because the friends who really care are the ones who don't save the ice cream for only celebrations. Devastating days are hard to slog through alone, and heart friends aren't scared of or embarrassed by your tears.

In fact, she might even have some tears of her own when

she sees your hurt. Heart friends don't skip out when life gets messy. They stick it out because true friendship is loyal even when there's nothing that can be done to fix the situation.

Friendship isn't about finding someone who's perfect. That person doesn't exist. But there are people in the world who will draw out the best in us and love us for who we are even as they encourage us to get stronger and be better.

Maybe you've heard it said that to have a good friend, you have to be a good friend. There's a lot of truth in that. The kind of people who speak truth and celebrate success with others aren't going to be vulnerable with people who love lies and tear others down.

If you're waiting for a heart friend to be a part of your life, keep your eyes open. Work on being a better friend and a healthier person. And ask God to bring a person into your life who will help you catch a glimpse of his heart for you every single day.

Live

Think about your circle of friends. What sort of habits do you all have? How do you act when you're together? Are your friends influencing you toward excellence or toward unhealthy things? Are you influencing your friends in some way? Maybe you don't have a friend you'd consider a heart friend, much less a circle of friends. Keep asking God to provide, and keep watch!

Pray

Dear Jesus, I want the kind of friends who will help me love you better and help me become the woman you created me to be. Would you point out the people already in my life who have the potential to become these friends to me? Would you bring someone into my life who will be a heart friend? Help me also to be the kind of friend who's able to love others this way too. I want to help my friends focus on you and how much you love them. Show me specific ways I can do this better and more often.

Think

A person with a heart for others truly loves them by continually pointing them back to Jesus, no matter the situation.

What Does It Mean to Love My Enemies?

"You have heard that it was said, 'Love your neighbor and hate your enemy.' But I tell you, love your enemies and pray for those who persecute you, that you may be children of your Father in heaven. He causes his sun to rise on the evil and the good, and sends rain on the righteous and the unrighteous. If you love those who love you, what reward will you get? Are not even the tax collectors doing that? And if you greet only your own people, what are you doing more than others? Do not even pagans do that?"

MATTHEW 5:43–47

Corrie ten Boom's family had a watch-making shop in Holland before World War II. But once Nazis began to round up Jews in her neighborhood, the shop was turned into a refuge for all who fled. Eventually, the entire ten Boom family was betrayed by a man who tricked them into believing he needed help, and they were arrested and imprisoned in concentration camps.

Corrie's father died shortly after being taken to prison. Corrie and her sister, Betsie, were taken to another prison, Ravensbruck, where they endured humiliation, torture, and terror at the hands of the guards. Betsie died there. Corrie was released shortly afterward because of a clerical error.

Years later, at a church service, Corrie saw one of the guards who had heaped torture upon her and her sister. She forgave him, but it wasn't as simple as just saying the words, because forgiveness isn't simple. For Corrie, and for all of us, forgiveness requires God's work in our hearts. She was only able to extend forgiveness to the guard because she begged God to help her do so.

It isn't that Corrie didn't experience anger or hurt because of all that had happened to her, her family, and all the oppressed, but she didn't let it keep her from being obedient to God. God asked her to forgive and love her enemies; she asked him for the love necessary to carry that out. In her book, *The Hiding Place*, Corrie wrote about her life and her continued journey toward forgiveness.

We haven't been imprisoned in concentration camps, but we all need to forgive. No matter what the circumstances, our need to forgive remains as important. Certainly, we've all wanted to heap hurt back into the lives of someone who's dumped pain over us. But seeking revenge is like giving our sin a megaphone and permission to be louder than Jesus in our lives.

Instead, to live life to the fullest, we need to heed the words of Jesus in Matthew 5:43–45: "You have heard that it was said, 'Love your neighbor and hate your enemy.' But I tell you, love your enemies and pray for those who persecute you, that you may be children of your Father in heaven." He's making it clear here that the way we treat our neighbors and the way we treat our enemies should look no different from each other. We're to love them both out loud. Our enemies became our enemies because they've shown us the worst of themselves. If we show them the worst of ourselves in return, it only puts our sin on display and hurts us further. Sin cannot blot out sin. Only love can do that.

Forgiving isn't easy. Forgiving and loving someone we consider an enemy often feels impossible.

For instance, it's easy to love adorable babies and cute puppies. They haven't done anything to hurt us! But forgiving and loving the person who betrayed us or put us in danger? That takes a kind of love we simply can't muster up on our own, the kind of love we gain only by being near God's heart and trusting what he has to say instead of what's going on around us. His example is perfect, so we learn from him.

When Jesus was crucified, he didn't call down fire from heaven and smite every centurion around, though he very well could have. He prayed for those who hurt him, the ones who took his life. He offered forgiveness to them, even when they didn't ask for it and even when they refused it. He preached the gospel to them by remaining true to God all the way through to his last breath.

After witnessing Jesus' love on the cross, a nearby centurion knew he'd encountered God, and it changed his heart. Actively loving our enemies is one of the greatest opportunities we have to show the rest of the world who we belong to and how he changes everything.

It takes a lot of wisdom and discernment to react in love toward our enemies when they've hurt us. It might not always seem clear to us how to extend love and forgiveness best. All situations are different, so we stick close to God's heart and ask him to guide us as we live. He says he'll give us wisdom when we ask for it. So, before we take any action at all, we seek his heart and ask him to show us what it looks like for us to love our enemies right now.

When we do the hard work of loving our enemies, it does something to our hearts that only God can do. Isaiah 61 says he makes beauty from ashes, garments of praise from our despair. Reacting in a way that's pleasing to God is like setting up a spike for our friend when we're playing volleyball. He uses our efforts to drive home his purposes. He uses our encounters with our enemies to make us more like him and to show the rest of the world the truth of his love.

Live

Did somebody immediately come to mind when you read the word *enemy*? What's the most loving thing you could do for that person today? How does your heart feel when you think of loving them?

Pray

Dear Lord, today I pray for my enemy by name. Please give me wisdom to know how to navigate the situation with (name). I feel angry and upset when I think of them, and I don't understand why it seems like they're able to continue living their lives without consequence while I deal with the mess they've made in my life. Help me to deal with my hurt feelings and to forgive this person for the things that caused me to think of them as an enemy. Bring healing to my heart where they have inflicted damage, and help me to love them out of that healing.

Think

A person has a heart for others when they love their enemies by seeking the best for them instead of exacting or even wanting revenge.

Having a Heart of Forgiveness

> Therefore, as God's chosen people, holy and dearly loved, clothe yourselves with compassion, kindness, humility, gentleness and patience. Bear with each other and forgive one another if any of you has a grievance against someone. Forgive as the Lord forgave you. And over all these virtues put on love, which binds them all together in perfect unity.
>
> **COLOSSIANS 3:12–14**

Forgiveness is a choice we all have to make at some point in our lives, and it's usually not a one-time decision. It takes concentrated effort to convince our hearts to stay with it, to cling to and lean into forgiveness.

Forgiveness is a whole-person matter, but often our hearts need to take the plunge before the rest of us will follow, and at times our hearts can be the most difficult to convince to forgive. Some of us have been grievously wounded by people who acted out against us to devastating results. Even seemingly simple daily digs have a way of grinding our souls down and causing us to forget whose we are and how much we matter.

It's easy to say we'll be happier and more whole if we can just forgive, but knowing it needs to happen is the easiest part of forgiveness. Making the actual choice, and being able to carry it through, feels more impossible than placing toothpaste back into the tube after it's already been used to brush your teeth.

Just like we can do nothing to earn the forgiveness God freely gives us, we can't demand that the people who've wronged us need to earn our forgiveness. It's an enormous sacrifice to offer forgiveness to another person. Can you think of a time someone hurt you and you truly thought they *deserved* your forgiveness? We'd really like to hold on to our anger and hurt, because then it feels like we're doing something productive in a situation where it seems like we have no control. But like many other paradoxes we'll encounter in our faith journeys, it's in the letting go of that control that we get back the freedom our hearts so desperately need after being injured.

God knows forgiveness is one of the most difficult things we'll do. He's not asking us to forgive because he likes to watch us suffer or because he loves to watch us try and fail to do impossible things. He understands sacrifice very well, and he specializes in taking what we offer to him, transforming it with his goodness, and giving us something beautiful of himself in its place.

We trust God to be who he says he is, a God of justice, so we can have faith that he cares deeply about the times we've been wronged. He knows every detail of what happens and every detail of how the event affects our hearts. So when he asks us to forgive those who've hurt us, it's not a light or flippant ask. It's a lifesaving, loving plea for our well-being.

He's the only one worthy of that ask too. Nobody else will ever have the right to suggest we must do such an audacious thing as letting go of our right to retaliate when we've been wronged. He's the only one who's been sinned against over and over again, and he always forgives.

In other words, God isn't asking us to do something he doesn't well understand. He wouldn't ask us to forgive if it wasn't necessary for our well-being or for our relationships with him. When we offer forgiveness to others, we're living out on earth the heavenly reality of God's forgiveness of our sins, the things we've done to betray and wound him.

The forgiveness God gives us, though, means we also have a restored relationship with him. This isn't always true of the relationships we have with those we forgive and those who've forgiven us. Restoration may not come until eternity in some cases. Trust was broken and ties were severed when the sin happened, and that sin still has consequences even after forgiveness. In cases of abuse or in situations where we feel unsafe around the other person, we don't need to rush back into a relationship with them to prove we're the forgiving type.

Forgiveness is a decision we make to allow God to hold that person accountable for their actions, a way to trust him as the source of justice and release ourselves from the burden of bitterness. We forgive because we're more obedient to God than we are to the people and situations Satan uses in an attempt to destroy us. Though forgiveness is never an easy thing to offer, it is the greatest gift we can give to anyone who wrongs us. And, also, maybe one of the greatest gifts we can give to our own hearts.

Live

Do you need to seek forgiveness from another person today? Or do you need to forgive someone for something that wounded your heart?

Maybe a person came to mind as soon as you read the title of this section, and your heart rebelled at the thought of truly forgiving that person. Remember, forgiveness is a choice. There are often layers to it that we may uncover over time. Take the first step of forgiveness today by offering your hurt and your need to retaliate to God. Give him your ashes, and see what beauty he gives in response.

Pray

Dear Jesus, forgiveness feels like an impossibly big thing to ask of me. You saw what that person did to me, and you know how much I hurt over those actions. But I don't want to be tied to that person by bitterness or unforgiveness anymore.

Today, I want to hand over my need to control the situation by holding on to unforgiveness. I trust you to demand consequences for that person's actions as you see fit. Help me to choose to embrace your compassion and care for me more than I grab on to my anger and pain.

Think

A heart that dwells in unforgiveness is a heart that cannot experience life to the fullest.

Can Confrontation Be Done in Love?

Brothers and sisters, if someone is caught in a sin, you who live by the Spirit should restore that person gently. But watch yourselves, or you also may be tempted. Carry each other's burdens, and in this way you will fulfill the law of Christ. If anyone thinks they are something when they are not, they deceive themselves. Each one should test their own actions. Then they can take pride in themselves alone, without comparing themselves to someone else, for each one should carry their own load.

GALATIANS 6:1–5

When you hear the word *confrontation*, what comes to mind? Maybe a lot of yelling. Possibly people throwing things and slamming doors. Some name-calling and anger. If you plug *confrontation* into a thesaurus, the related words that come up are things like *hostility* and *battle*. These are unpleasant words, things that describe pain and destruction. Truthfully, though, pain and destruction are exactly what most of us think about when we're faced with a conversation that will include confrontation.

Confrontation is one of those things most of us avoid, so it seems odd that we could have a conversation about potentially volatile topics and still feel loved and affirmed later on. But confrontation is something we need to learn to do really well if we want to be able to love our friends fully over many years.

Even in the godliest friendships, feelings are bound to get hurt. Sometimes those moments are minor missteps and we move on without incident. Other times, real damage happens, and we can't move on until the situation is resolved.

Maybe it would help if we tossed out the word *confrontation*. It really does make us think of anger more than love, and that's not the spirit we want going into a conversation with someone we care about, even if it's about an unpleasant topic. Galatians 6:1 has a beautiful way of talking about what happens when it's necessary to call out another believer who has sinned. It says to "restore that person gently."

When centuries-old paintings need to be restored, art galleries and museum curators don't call in anyone with a set of paints. They hire a restoration artist, someone who has respect for the original artwork and the skills to call out its original beauty, to make sure the original artist's intent isn't lost to the rest of the world. A good restoration artist, no matter how skillful, would never paint over a piece with her own artwork because that would ruin the integrity of the piece.

We go into difficult conversations with the people we love the same way—with a mindset and spirit of restoration, respecting the individuality and beauty that's already there. Sometimes their beauty may seem deeply hidden, especially when they've deeply wounded us. But every person, no matter how far we've wandered from our Creator's original intent, still carries the imprint of his spirit. There's no room for our own entitlement or a better-than-you attitude when we have hard conversations with others. Instead, we call out the behavior *and* the beauty we know still exists in that person, reminding her of our Maker's original intent.

This sounds sweet and serene, doesn't it? Unfortunately, though, even when our motives are to bring restoration to the situation in a loving and kind way, things still go sideways. Who likes a friend telling them they've done something hurtful or sinful? It's like a spear directly to our hearts, cutting right to our deepest sense of ourselves.

That's why it's absolutely necessary to examine our own hearts before we have the conversation with our friend in need of a nudge. If there's anything in our own hearts that's less than pure, we need to address that before going to our friends. Galatians 6 also reminds us to "watch [ourselves]" and to "test [our] own actions." Satan doesn't need extra ammo to lob at our life-giving friendships, so we do our best to clear that stuff away before we decide to step into hard conversations.

Our hearts are just as important as the hearts of the people we approach. Rushing into a conversation with the intent to scold or shame another person into submission is exactly how we find ourselves right back in hostile confrontation territory. We'll never be perfect, of course, but a humble heart promotes healing more than one that's puffed up and arrogant.

Sometimes we're the ones who need to be restored. We're just as capable of falling into sin and patterns of destruction as everyone else. Hopefully we're surrounded by trustworthy people who are willing to point us back toward restoration in a loving manner, but we have to be sure our hearts are tender and receptive to those conversations. If someone we trust comes to us with a concern, we listen!

The kind of relationships that allow these authentic interactions are rare and good treasures. Proverbs 27:6 says, "Wounds from a friend can be trusted, but an enemy multiplies kisses." When a true friend approaches us with wise critique, we can prayerfully consider what she has to say. Enemies rely on flattery and pretend everything's okay even when damage festers below the surface, but true friends know healing is worth the temporary pain of cleaning out the wound.

We can't be the kind of women who point out areas in need of change in others' lives and refuse to believe we don't often need the same support as well. Nor can we be the kind of women willing to let sin take over our friendships and eat away at them like an infection.

With wisdom, prayer, and heaps of grace, we can be women who are gentle and authentic enough to speak the truth *and* hear it when it comes back to us.

Live

How do you feel when you think about having difficult conversations with your friends? Have these types of restorations happened in your life before? Did it go well, or did it go poorly? Do you think you'd be open to a conversation about your heart's need for change with a godly friend?

Pray

Dear Lord, I don't want to be the kind of person who can only see sin when it's in the lives of other people. If there's anything in me pulling my heart away from you, please point it out and show me what the root of that sin is. And before I take concerns about another person's spiritual health to them, remind me to pause and take care of my own heart first. Help my heart to stay soft and moldable, even when I may need to say or hear tough things.

Think

A person with a heart for others approaches her friends after she's examined herself, in order to help her friends be restored to the original intent of their Creator.

Loving Others from the Overflow of My Heart

A good man brings good things out of the good stored up in his heart, and an evil man brings evil things out of the evil stored up in his heart. For the mouth speaks what the heart is full of.

LUKE 6:45

The contents of a vessel matter. For instance, I'd love to have an overflowing bowl of ice cream. I would not in any way love to have an overflowing toilet bowl.

Our hearts are the most important vessel we have, and every day we make choices that fill it up either with great things that give us life or with terrible things that destroy us. Sometimes we trick ourselves into thinking that as long as we keep the contents of our heart a secret, nobody else will ever find out.

But Jesus has something to say about that. "A good man brings good things out of the good stored up in his heart," Jesus says in Luke 6:45. "And an evil man brings evil things out of the evil stored up in his heart. For the mouth speaks what the heart is full of." Anything we put into our hearts comes out in the way we live our lives. The more junk that goes into our hearts, the more that junk overflows in the things we say and the way we treat other people. It won't stay hidden, no matter how hard we try to cover it up and no matter how successful we think we are. God isn't tricked by our deception, even if we buy into it ourselves.

When we can't love other people, it's because we have a heart problem. What we've poured into our hearts has created an environment that's unfit for love to thrive. On the other hand, when we *do* love others, it's because we've spent time with and have been changed by God, who is love. He gives of himself, filling our hearts with everything we need to dip into as we love and serve each other.

We don't need more of ourselves or more of our own goodness to pour out. Our goodness might benefit others for a moment, and that's great, but what's most important is that other people experience God's goodness. We need more of Jesus.

To love people well, we need to take care of our spiritual well-being. There's no substitute for a relationship with Jesus, and there are no shortcuts to a healthy relationship with him. We have to read his Word to get to know his heart for us and his heart for others. We have to spend time in prayer so we can recognize when he answers and so he can instruct and change our hearts. It's not that we need to do these things just because they're what "good Christians" do. We do these things because our hearts won't thrive without them. On our own, we'll love people for a short time, then get burned out because we have nothing left, since we've not been spending regular time with the source of all Love. If we haven't learned from God or experienced life with him, then we can't share him with anybody.

Have you ever thought it was odd how Jesus stepped away from the crowd at times? There are several occasions when he withdrew, leaving the mobs of followers behind. Often, he would take this time away to connect with God through prayer. If it was necessary for Jesus to continue meeting with God on a regular basis as he loved and served people, it's certainly even more necessary for us.

To love people well, we need to take care of our physical well-being. Our bodies aren't invincible. If we neglect caring for ourselves, our bodies pay the price. It serves no one if we've run ourselves ragged and become so exhausted we can no longer function. God cares about rest and how we integrate it into our lives, so much so that he modeled it for us during creation. On the seventh day, he rested, even though he hadn't grown physically tired.

We, too, have to carve out time to rest even when it seems like others would be better served if we kept doing. Even when we rest, God keeps working. His plans aren't dependent on our power and our ability to keep up—it's only because of him that any plan is carried out. Rest allows us to remember that God is truly the one in control. None of our relationships, none of our dreams, none of our love for others is dependent on our constant performance.

To love people well, we need to take care of our mental well-being. It's obvious that our hearts play a big role in caring for others, but we might forget our minds need to be constantly renewed as well. Romans 12:2 tells us to "be transformed by the renewing of [our] mind[s]." Our minds aren't stagnant pieces of ourselves that get put on autopilot as soon as we're able to put together sentences. We continuously grow and change and learn new things as we get older.

Sometimes we learn the wrong things. People make statements about us that are untrue, but they stick anyway. We're hurt by a family member and make an unconscious vow to never allow ourselves to be in a similar situation where we could be betrayed again. Whatever has happened to us, we've learned some patterns that keep us from being able to love well.

It's our responsibility as the keepers of our hearts and minds to take stock of these bad lessons and call them out. Are we still storing them up in our hearts? If so, they get in the way when we try to love. They obscure our perception of other people and keep us from loving with pure hearts.

Everything in our hearts spills out when we're in relationship with other people. We get to choose whether we'll spend our lives pouring evil into the world (which seems like it already has enough of that . . .) or pouring Jesus' goodness and love into thirsty hearts instead.

Live

Is your heart overflowing, dry, or somewhere in between today? Which area of your well-being do you need to pay attention to in order to get back to (or maintain) that overflowing level? When you take stock of what you're storing in your heart, what do you think of first? If you asked the people in your life what you love and how that's reflected in your life, what would they say?

Pray

Dear Lord, I know I'm not invincible. When I start to get depleted, would you tug on my heart and remind me to return to you for refreshment? Help me store only your goodness and love in my heart, and teach me to let go of the rest. You've given me abundance, and I want to show others how they can have that in their own lives as well. That can only happen if I stay connected with you, so help me to do that every day.

Think

A Christ follower that loves others knows that the source of her love comes from Jesus alone.

My Changed Heart Changes the World

When Jesus looked up and saw a great crowd coming toward him, he said to Philip, "Where shall we buy bread for these people to eat?" He asked this only to test him, for he already had in mind what he was going to do.

Philip answered him, "It would take more than half a year's wages to buy enough bread for each one to have a bite!"

Another of his disciples, Andrew, Simon Peter's brother, spoke up, "Here is a boy with five small barley loaves and two small fish, but how far will they go among so many?"

JOHN 6:5–9

Did you know there are over 7.6 billion people on Earth right now? It's true—you can google it for a live count if you want to watch the numbers in real time. And you're just one of those 7.6 billion and climbing. Is there anything one of us can do that could possibly make a difference with numbers like that? On days when it feels like it's "me against the world," it seems like the answer to that question is a loud, resounding NO.

We'd love to end extreme global poverty, but we make ten dollars an hour babysitting. Ten dollars an hour isn't going to put a dent in that enormous problem. It would be awesome to get the thousands of kids in our states out of the foster care system and into safe, loving homes, but our parents aren't on board.

It makes no sense that people in America and all around the world are trafficked and tricked into slavery, but we can't storm brothels and physically rescue people.

While there are things we can do to help a lot of people, sometimes it still doesn't feel like very much given everything else that needs to be done.

Don't you wonder if the young man hanging out by the Sea of Galilee around Passover time felt the same way? He's only mentioned once in one of the Gospels, the book of John. As far as we know, he was just a totally normal guy spending time around Jesus.

Jesus asks (even though he already knows what he's about to do), "Where shall we buy bread for these people to eat?" The disciples scrambled. Philip panicked over the finances. And in chapter six, verse nine, Andrew pulls the boy out of the gathering crowd and says words that must have been life changing for the kid: "Here is a boy with five small barley loaves and two small fish, but how far will they go among so many?"

How often do we ask God the same kind of question? "But, Lord, I'm just a girl with a few small ideas and an even smaller budget. How far will those things go among so many? How can I, one person, make any difference in a world of over 7.6 billion?"

Jesus didn't laugh at the young man's offering of bread and fish. He used it to make a miracle a reality for five thousand people. He doesn't laugh at our ideas or our small budget or anything else we offer him, either. Even though the needs in the world seem infinite and overwhelming, we can believe in the power of our God, who actually *is* infinite and totally in control. He doesn't need us to work ourselves into a frenzy to give him more and more and more. He asks us to give him what we already have. Jesus doesn't need more stuff or more resources—everything already belongs to him. But he wants us to participate.

We need to remember the two things the young man had if we want to participate in the work Jesus is already doing. The boy was near Jesus, and he was willing to give what he had to Jesus.

We need to stay near Jesus. The young man was physically next to Jesus. He'd followed Jesus and was close by when there was a need that Jesus could fill.

We can't be physically close to Jesus these days, but that doesn't mean we can't be near him. If we're Christ followers, we have the Holy Spirit with us. He's present with us all the time. Though he never hides or moves away from us, we sometimes move away from him when we're wooed by rebellion or if we feel ashamed or guilty. Sin is a human condition, and we're all human, after all. None of us is too good or too righteous to be immune.

To stay near to Jesus, we constantly need to be on guard and vigilant, ready to call out the slightest sins in our lives. We don't do this out of a heart of legalism, but out of a heart that wants *nothing* to get in the way of our nearness to Christ. If we want to be active participants in the work of Jesus, we need to be able to concentrate on him without distraction. So we throw away our sin and pursue him with all our hearts, spending time getting to know him through prayer, through his Word, and through time spent with other Christ followers.

We willingly offer what we already have to Jesus. What would have happened if the young man had hoarded his resources? We don't know much of his story from Scripture, but what if he had the five loaves and two fish because he hadn't eaten breakfast that morning and he was really hungry? Or what if he'd planned on taking it home to his younger siblings? Many of us might have been tempted to tuck the bread and the fish back under our robes before going home.

But this young man willingly offered what he already had. It was surely a sacrifice on his part. It doesn't look like he had a special "in" with the Lord. Even the disciples flipped out a little bit when Jesus asked them to find dinner because they didn't know where it would come from.

Jesus took what was given to him, broke it and blessed it, then gave it back more than five thousand times over to supply his miraculous provision to the crowd. Later on in John, it says that after the people saw what Jesus had done, they said, "Surely this is the Prophet who is to come into the world." Because the young man offered what he had, many saw the power of Jesus with their own eyes that day.

When we willingly offer whatever we have, even if what we have seems small or insignificant, God takes it, breaks it, blesses it, and uses it. We can only do so much with what we've been given, but he is able to do far more than we could ever ask or imagine.

Live

Have you ever felt like what you have is too little to offer? There's nothing too little to use in God's economy. What's required of us is the offering. He takes care of the rest! What's one offering you can make today?

Pray

Dear Jesus, I'm excited, honestly. It's incredible to think you care about what I have to give. I know all the good things I have today are blessings from the palms of your hands, and I want to give those things back to you. Right now I have (a dream, a certain amount of time, some money—you choose what applies to your life!), and I want to offer that back to you. Maybe I've been holding back before now because it seemed too small to make a difference. But I know you use even small things to make a big impact for your kingdom, and I want you to be in charge of that from now on.

Think

A Christ follower offers whatever she has back to God so that he can take it, break it, bless it, and pour it out to change the world.

Now and Not Yet

Therefore we do not lose heart. Though outwardly we are wasting away, yet inwardly we are being renewed day by day. For our light and momentary troubles are achieving for us an eternal glory that far outweighs them all. So we fix our eyes not on what is seen, but on what is unseen, since what is seen is temporary, but what is unseen is eternal.

2 CORINTHIANS 4:16–18

Do you or did you ever have braces? It's one of those rites of passage many of us must go through. At first it seems exciting. You can match your rubber bands to your favorite sports team's colors! Or to the nearest holiday! But then the orthodontist tightens things up, and it gets a lot less fun real fast. Who cares about the colors when the only things you can eat anymore are pudding and scrambled eggs, at least until your mouth adjusts to its new normal?

But the tightening of the wires and brackets is necessary. To have a straight, healthy smile and bite at the end of the process, there must be tension. The pain is a constant reminder that your teeth aren't where they are meant to be, but they're on the way there.

It's so like our lives, isn't it? We aren't where we're meant to be, but we're on the way there. There's pain too, which reminds us along the way. The pain usually shows up as undeniable tension and hard questions without easy answers.

If God is good, then why does he let truly terrible things happen? Why, if I loved others like Jesus said, did my former best friend turn around and betray me? If God actually answers prayer, then how come it seems like my prayers go unanswered?

Those questions are all echoes of a bigger theme that arches over our whole faith journey: Jesus was the living sacrifice that restored our relationship with God the Father, and now we wait for him to come back and make all things right. We've seen the greatest good in Jesus, and we've also seen terrible evil and hardship in the world today. All wrongs haven't been righted.

Yet.

It's so easy to forget about that *yet.* We stare at divorce and disease and death, and it's hard to look away. It's hard to remember God exists—much less that he's in love with us and carries us near to his heart—when the rest of the world and even our own experiences work overtime to convince us otherwise. But those things don't get the last word!

Outwardly, we're wasting away. Life is really uncomfortable sometimes because of sin and its influence in our world. But the discomfort and the pain doesn't diminish who God is and what he's promised for us, what's he's set aside for our futures. He is still who he says he is in spite of every single ounce of darkness that touches our lives. God is absolutely trustworthy.

When we trust God to be true to himself no matter what we're going through, it sets off a chain of events that tightens the space between him and us. Our faith in Jesus increases. We're pulled nearer to his heart and nearer to the women he created us to be for his glory.

Hard, bad things happen, and Satan hopes these things will drive us farther from God's heart. He's counting on us to feel the tension of unanswered, hard questions, to hurt, and to turn away because of them. Lots of people do. Do you have friends or family members who've gone through a seriously tough time and decided they didn't want anything to do with God afterward? It happens.

But it doesn't have to happen to us. Remember, tension hurts when we're wearing braces, but it's necessary and helpful in pulling our smile together, where it's supposed to be. The tension we live in right now, where God is absolutely *good* but our circumstances are still absolutely *awful,* is instrumental in pulling us back to Christ if we don't walk away before the process is over. And the process for us won't be over until we're in eternity with Jesus.

We have lots of questions, and God's given us the freedom to ask them. He's not afraid of our hurting hearts, and he's not afraid of questions that don't have easy answers. We don't need to be afraid of them either.

Because we trust in God, we don't need to be afraid of our pain or our hard-to-answer questions either. Just because we don't have the answers, it doesn't mean he's not listening. We can accept the tension and the discomfort of today because we believe there's peace and healing to come. "So we fix our eyes not on what is seen, but on what is unseen," 2 Corinthians says, "since what is seen is temporary, but what is unseen is eternal."

Ask the hard questions. Take a long, close look at the tension and the pain in the world today. Those things exist, and they're real and need to be dealt with, grieved, and fought over in our hearts. But they're also temporary, and they're useful in pulling us nearer to God's heart.

Tension can rip things apart too. Isn't that what we usually think of when we hear the word, anyway? Great chasms and splitting apart and irreconcilable differences. But it's our choice that makes the difference. If we choose to fight against the tension, we'll be pulled apart, ripped away. But if we lean into it and let it do the work instead, we'll eventually be drawn together, put back in place where we belong, in step with the heart of God.

Do not lose heart, dear friend. Because of God's magnificent, incredible, forever love for you, there are greater things to come. In the meantime, let your smile be bright, and keep watch for his light on the horizon. He's on his way for us.

Live

What have you been fixing your eyes on lately? Remind yourself right now of who God is and how he feels about you. In spite of the hard questions and the tough times, he remains unchanged, and so does his love for you.

Pray

Dear Jesus, I'm so thankful that what I see now isn't what lasts forever. Make my heart soft and receptive to all the ways you draw me near, even if sometimes that requires tension and unanswered questions. Help me lean into you and allow the tension to pull me closer to your heart. I want my heart and my smile and everything about me to reflect your love to a hurting world. I don't want to lose heart. Instead, I want to be close to yours.

Think

A person with a heart for others remembers where she is right now and how that compares to what is in store for her in eternity.